Why Do Good People Suffer?

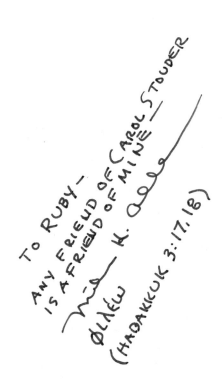

To Ruby —
Any friend of Carol Stouder
is a friend of mine
Olaew H. ____
(Habakkuk 3:17,18)

WHY DO GOOD PEOPLE SUFFER?

Milton H. Allen

BROADMAN PRESS
Nashville, Tennessee

1983

4252-08
ISBN: 0-8054-5208-7

Dewey Decimal Classification: 223.2
Subject heading: SUFFERING
Library of Congress Catalog Card Number: 82-82949
Printed in the United States of America

Dedicated to the memory of my mother,
Rachel Lizabeth Allen,
with whom, through the kindness of my church, I was able to spend a great number of hours in the hospital prior to her death. These days and nights of vigil provided me with the much-needed time and inspiration to rethink my ideas concerning suffering. I would normally not have had this opportunity in the midst of my regular pastoral duties. This brought home, in a very personal way, one of the main themes of this book, that there is compensation in suffering.

Foreword

Suffering is the common lot of all mankind. At all times, and in all places, people have sought to find answers to its meaning. Volumes have been written on the subject.

In one way or another all religions include suffering as part of their "stock in trade." The Bible itself is a book concerned with suffering. The Book of Job deals primarily with the subject.

The Christian faith is wedded to the theme of suffering. Christianity was founded by a "Suffering Messiah." He was a man of sorrows and acquainted with grief (Isa. 53:3). And he is not only the prime example of suffering, but he is the best example of how we are to overcome it.

The "why" of suffering could be included as one of the basic questions asked about life. All people have at one time or another puzzled over life and asked: "Where did we come from?" "Why are we here?" "Where are we going?" To this list could be added the additional question: "Why do we suffer?"

In mankind's search for the meaning of suffering, surprisingly few answers have been found. Despite the various ways to suffer, the reasons behind suffering seem to be limited to a few basic ideas. They can be listed under a few general headings: punishment, purification, a sharing experience, without purpose but with compensation, testing, and so forth.

In this book I have tried to take these ideas and approach them in a practical and simple way. I have sought to illustrate these reasons with a number of personal and general anecdotes collected from various sources.

This book is not meant to be a complete treatment on the subject of suffering. It is written more as a practical help—perhaps, one could say, a handbook.

The Bible quotations used throughout the book are mostly from the King James Version. This translation was chosen because of its popularity and availability to most readers. Other versions should be used to clarify passages or words.

Contents

Introduction

From the first sharp cry when the newborn baby gulps its first breath until the last gasp at the end of life, a person suffers. People come into this world through the pain of birth and leave it through the pain of death.

The joy of childhood is jostled by pain. The happiness of youth is often marred by the heartbreak of young love and the anguish of adjusting to life. Middle age is filled with the conflict of uncertainty amid a challenge of change. Old age brings with it the sorrow of solitude and the sadness of separation.

Beginning at birth and continuing through life, a person is always a participant in suffering and not just a spectator. Suffering stands, with sword drawn, waiting for a person at every crossroad. Suffering is met at every turn. It reaches out and touches both sinner and saint alike. To all people it comes, not equally, but inevitably. No one is exempt.

For some, suffering is a constant companion, like the proverbial "albatross about their neck."[1] They must bear it either bravely or begrudgingly. For some it attacks without warning, like a thief in the night. To others, it slithers in slowly like a serpent, striking, and poisoning them in body and spirit. "Man that is born of a woman is of few days, and full of trouble" (Job 14:1). This is the way Job, in the Old Testament, summed it all up.

The fact of suffering is not in question. Regardless of how positive we think or how strong our will, we cannot cloud its presence. The question is never, "Does a person suffer?" But always, "Why does a person suffer?"

No one knows the full meaning behind all suffering. It eludes us. It is far too complicated for anyone to fully understand or explain. There are multiple and overlapping causes and reasons for suffering. There are no easy or "pat" answers.

The best that can be said about the meaning of suffering is that "we see through a glass, darkly." We only "know in part" (1 Cor. 13:12). God alone knows all the reasons. However, out of this darkness a pattern does emerge; and, if we will strain to look, we can clearly see that there is design.

It has been said that human beings can tolerate almost anything if they can find purpose behind it. If a reason for suffering is seen, a person can usually bear it. However, if a person feels that personal suffering is the result of blind, impersonal chance or fate, he quickly succumbs to despair. One of the reasons political wars are so frustrating is at this very point: meaning is clouded and lost; goals are ill defined; purpose is perverted. It is not that men die, but that they seem to die so uselessly.

Likewise, the main reason why suffering becomes so unbearable to many is that they see no purpose behind it. They see no "rhyme or reason" in the universe and thus no meaning to life and to suffering. This is why the answer to suffering is so closely allied with religion. To face suffering and to overcome it requires a God-centered philosophy of life in a God-controlled universe. Religion alone seems to provide the faith to interpret suffering and the power to rise above it.

The Bible tells us that there is meaning behind the mystery of suffering. And not only meaning, but there can be joy and victory over it rather than just acceptance. The lives of many great Christian saints have shown this to be true.

In this book my aim is to show that suffering has purpose, that God is still on the throne and in control of the affairs of people. He knows all about us and cares for us as individuals. He can weave our suffering into the scheme of things for good. Suffering can be used by him to bless us and not curse us, and to fulfill his purpose.

Jesus was speaking literally when he said, "Are not five sparrows sold for two farthings, and not one of them is forgotten before God? But even the very hairs of your head are all numbered. Fear not therefore: ye are of more value than many sparrows" (Luke 12:6-7).

1

What's It All About?

What's it all about? What is suffering? As a word, *suffering* is hard to define. It is much easier to use one of its many synonyms. *Pain* is a word often used synonymously with suffering, yet suffering is not restricted to pain alone.

Pain is more correctly considered to be physical. In a narrow sense it is suffering caused by disease or injury. Pain may be suffering, but suffering is not always pain.

Usually the word *suffering* means an extreme or prolonged discomfort, and may either be mental or physical. For the purpose of this book, the word *suffering* will be used in a very broad sense; it will mean anything undesirable or unpleasant—the opposite of what we consider to be enjoyment at the time.

Of course, when we begin to define terms, we run into a problem immediately. What one person considers to be suffering might not be thought of as suffering by another. Both might experience the same thing but interpret it differently, or in different degrees. In physical suffering this is called a "threshold of pain," and implies that one can endure more than another. The same is also true of mental and emotional suffering, where one's degree of toleration may vary.

For a few people, even the line between pain and pleasure is not always clearly defined. The word *masochist* is used for those who receive a sense of pleasure through pain. The word today is not restricted to pain in the context of sexual pleasure. Then there is the "sadist" who receives pleasure through the suffering of others. Here, too, the word is no longer confined to the area of sex. Sometimes people in positions of authority or power can be sadists. They like to "lord it over" those under them by causing unnecessary hardships or even pain.

Some people, in a perverted way of thinking, would even accuse God of being a sadist. How wrong! Just the opposite is true. God is in the other column of the ledger: he suffers when his children suffer. When parents watch their children writhe in pain or waste away on a hospital bed, they are suffering. (In some immeasurable way they may be suffering more than the child.) God suffers, too, as he identifies with mankind's suffering. Since God is described as a loving Father, he too experiences suffering like a parent. There is no question but the Heavenly Father suffered while his own Son was on the cross. But all of this will be covered more fully in another chapter.

Consider another example where the line of suffering is not clearly drawn: the "stoic." Perhaps in his attempt to be indifferent to both pleasure and pain, he may be receiving some form of satisfaction from his suffering, even a form of pleasure in his stoicism.

The "martyr," who is willing to sacrifice his life for a principle, is in a sense experiencing a union of suffering and pleasure. Though his present experience of suffering is real, he may not consider it to be so in view of the future reward or the glory that will be his. The martyr is more than willing to suffer something bad in order to gain something good, or give up something good to have something better—even his short earthly life for everlasting life.

In comparing the losses in this life with the gain in the next, the apostle Paul wrote, "For I reckon that the sufferings of this present time are not worthy to be compared with the glory which shall be revealed in us" (Rom. 8:18).

Jesus taught that the kingdom of God is like this. In order to gain in one realm, one must suffer loss in another—the personal kingdom of self. He taught that the price of the kingdom of God was this very denial of self. Yet paradoxically, if one accepts this loss, one gains a greater self—an eternal self that can never be lost.

Jim Elliot, one of five martyred missionaries who died in South America a number of years ago caught this truth and expressed it clearly. After he surrendered his life to God's will and the mission field, he expressed his choice in this way: "He is no fool who gives that which he cannot keep to gain that which he can never lose."

Jesus said: "For whosoever will save his life shall lose it: and whosoever will lose his life for my sake shall find it" (Matt. 16:25). His parables of the pearl merchant and the hidden treasure illustrate this point well.

In the first story, Jesus told of a merchant looking for fine pearls. When the merchant found one of great value he did not hesitate to sell all his pearls in order to buy the one pearl (Matt. 13:45-46). In light of his gain he did not consider the sale of inferior pearls to be a loss.

In the other, he told of a farmer plowing in a leased field. As he turned over the soil he also turned over a hidden treasure. Immediately he covered it again and gladly went and sold everything he had and bought the field (Matt. 13:44). Again, in light of the treasure he was getting the farmer did not consider the sale of his possessions for the purchase of the field a sacrifice. He suffered a loss in one area but received a greater gain in another. His gain made the loss seem unimportant.

For these two men to have lost their possessions in a bad business deal would have been different. Or, had they lost their property through a natural calamity, their loss would have been called suffering. But to lose in order to gain brought them joy.

One wonders if much of our suffering is not like these two parables. God allows us to lose something good in order to gain something better. In the cases of the pearl merchant and the farmer, the gain was immediate. But in our suffering the gain may not be as quickly or as clearly seen. But the difference in time and our poor estimate of values does not minimize the parallel.

In a simple way we see this principle at work every day. Take the experience of eating, for example. We will probably enjoy our dinner much more if we miss lunch. To suffer the pangs of hunger in the afternoon only serves to increase our appreciation for dinner that evening. However, if we indulge our appetite thirty minutes before dinner with a double chocolate malted milk, then our dinner will not be enjoyed as much. On the other hand, the lack of enjoyment might be less painful than the scolding we might get for having so foolishly "ruined our appetite." So, we eat, suffer, and say nothing.

Anticipation is another area where pain can mingle with pleasure. Every hiker knows the joy of anticipation that comes with thirst. He can literally enjoy thirsting if he knows there is a spring of cool water just over the hill. In fact, men have died in the desert with water in their canteen because they saved their last drink for the satisfaction it would bring when they thought their thirst would be unbearable.

In the matter of suffering versus blessing, it is not easy to divide the two into separate camps. The lines are not well defined. They overlap and are entwined. The overall picture of suffering, along with the purpose behind it, plays an important part in its interpretation.

2

How Did It All Begin?

How did suffering get started? Where did it come from? Why is it here? And especially, why do good people suffer?

Since evil seems to be closely tied in with suffering, perhaps if we can find the answer to one, we will find the answer to the other. So, the question is: "Where did evil—and, thus suffering—come from?"

The first question we must answer in our search for the source of evil is this: "Is there a God who created all things?" We must begin here. Either there is a God or there is not. It is that simple, and that basic. Our answer to this question tells us how far we can go, and the direction we must take in our search.

If there is no God, the search ends! We can go no further. There is therefore no problem with evil or suffering for there is no meaning to either—but neither is there meaning to life. For without God we are not even allowed to ask the question, "Why do good people suffer?" For there are no good people, and there can be no purpose to suffering. Without God there is no plane of reference on which to establish either purpose or meaning.

Without God, life becomes only "a fool's nightmare."

It is a tale
Told by an idiot, full of sound and fury,
Signifying nothing.[1]

However, design stakes a claim to the truth that there must be a designer—God, and design implies purpose. A belief in God may have its questions, but the denial of God produces even more problems. Simply denying God doesn't solve anything, let alone provide an answer to design.

Most people cannot accept the idea of a world without a Creator. They believe there is too much design for this to have been a mere matter of chance. The world appears to be far more than a few atoms grouped together for a purposeless race through space. People are prone to despair if they cannot see hope and meaning in life. Without direction they soon find no reason for going on. Most agree with John Dryden:

> This is a piece too fair
> To be the child of chance, and not of Care.
> No atoms casually together hurl'd
> Could e'er produce so beautiful a world.[2]

If we are willing to accept the idea of a God, then the question that follows is, "What kind of a God?" Is he simply a "first cause," a "creative force" like energy? Or is he one who is concerned with his creation, and concerned about mankind? Is he a personal God?

Again, it seems there is far too much purpose in design for the Creator not to have "followed through." In other words, God personally rules over and intervenes in his creation. He seems to have taken too much "pains" with his creation to go off and leave it running by itself until finally, like a machine, it runs down. Somehow he is in the middle of it all, involved—a purposeful God.

Then is this personal God a good God? This naturally follows as the next question. And, it is at this point that things begin to "bog down." If God is a good God, then why does he allow evil and suffering? Does he send it? (It requires no great amount of intelligence to see that evil is with us. Even a child knows this. And he knows that it is not good.) If God is the Creator of all things, did he create evil? Is he personally responsible for suffering? If so, then how can he be regarded as a good God when suffering is not good? This is the whole crux of the matter. How can we harmonize a good God with suffering and evil? Despite this apparent dilemma there are ways to reconcile evil and suffering with a God who is good.

But, what is good? A person often feels a pressure to do right and to reject the bad. People seem to know what they "ought" to do. If the universe is indifferent to these values, then why this feeling toward good? Why this pressure to move toward the good?

Mankind elevates to the highest level such ideals as love and self-sacrifice. They are sensed to be good. Things like hate and cruelty are relegated to the lowest of levels. People know they are not good. Why this distinction?

There are those who feel that answering the question "Why is there good in the world?" could help us accept the idea of a good God.[3] Apart from a good God, mankind might be no better than the beasts of the earth. There seems to be no reason for heroes and people who give themselves to serve others without the goodness of the God who created it. So let us ask this question and see if we can find some answers.

Where did all this good come from if not from a good God? Perhaps it might be argued that mankind could develop a system of "good" independent of God. Certain standards of conduct could be established for dealing with one's neighbor. Laws might be made for the "good" of the majority, or to protect the individual. Then people who most nearly abided by these rules could be termed "good people." But the question still remains: What is the basis on which a person's "good" is established? Where did it come from? Why do people dare to presume that there is "goodness"?

If mankind, the created, can have this insight into good, then it follows that the Creator must be good. A fountain rises no higher than its source. The author must be greater than his work. That which is created cannot be better than its creator. Thus, it must follow that God is good. At their best, people certainly would not want to be the author of evil, so it is consistent to assume that the Creator of human beings would not either.

A second and valid argument for the goodness of God is the witness of millions who have come to know God in a very personal way through his Son, Jesus Christ. They all give testimony to the truth that they have found God, and that they have found him to be good. Their witness and testimony cannot be denied or ignored.

The Bible itself is a book about a good God who honors good and hates evil. It declares in word and example that God is good. And upon its pages is the story of Jesus Christ who came and revealed God in all of his goodness.

Jesus Christ was God who came to earth as a man in order for people to know him. So, to know him is to know God. And to know him is to know that God is good. God is so clearly revealed in Jesus Christ that the dullest of minds can understand that he is good.

Now, let me summarize. There is a God; he is creator; he is personal; he is concerned with his creation; and he is a good God. And, if he is good, then he did not create evil per se.

Then, if God is not the source of evil, where did it come from? The conclusion must be that evil came from some source other than God. But where? If God did not create evil, then, as the Creator of all things, he must have created something that had the ability to become evil.

Then why doesn't a good God stop evil? Is he powerless against it? No, God is all powerful. And evil is something God can stop but does not choose to do so—at least not just now. Instead, he is in the process of stopping it—forever. Consider the following story:

Imagine a scene in heaven long ago, before time began. There is one bright angel, brighter than all the rest, the brightest of all the created ones. He is standing in the corner of heaven discussing in whispered tones a matter of the greatest importance with some of the heavenly host.

"Look," he says, "have you ever wondered why you serve God?"

"We just do, that's all. We were made for that purpose," said one of the smaller angels.

"Because of love," came back another answer in a deep preaching tone. "He loves us and we love him."

"How do you know he loves you?" challenged the bright angel with a voice that would cause one to shudder.

"Well, we have always assumed that he did. We never questioned it. Doesn't he provide for our every need?" answered one of the angels rather meekly.

"A slave master would do that for his slaves," snapped the bright angel, looking enviously toward the throne.

"What would happen if you should exercise your 'God-given' freedom and refused to serve him?"

The other angels confessed they didn't know. They never had given it a thought. "Besides," they said, "we don't like to think about such things."

"Naturally," answered the bright one. "Do you know what he would do? He would destroy us all with a snap of his finger. He rules with an iron fist."

"No, no!" cried the whole group of angels in shocked disbelief.

"And that Son of his, strutting around heaven all day," continued the bright one, "he acts like he's better than the rest of the created host. I'll put my created beauty up against his eternal glory any day!"

The seeds of doubt were now sown! They would grow! The damage was done. A flag of rebellion was raised. God's holy authority had been challenged. To round up this horde of rebellious angels and destroy them would only give credence to the accuser's[4] argument. Yet, God could not have rebellion in heaven.

So God was on trial. His motive for ruling had been attacked. He ruled by love, surely everyone ought to know that, but somehow, he must allow the adversary[5] and his followers time for a fair hearing. To "strike them down" without a hearing would cause the faithful angels to wonder if perhaps this slanderer[6] was right. To destroy them without allowing this spirit of rebellion to "run its full course" would convince neither the loyal nor the rebellious. The seeds of rebellion must now be allowed to bear their bitter fruit.

But if they would not be ruled by God in heaven, then they must be free to rule themselves somewhere else. But where? They would not be permitted to remain in heaven.

"Down there," came the cry of the rebellious angel.

"Yes," was the overwhelming shout of his followers.

So, this proud and rebellious archangel, the defamer,[7] was expelled, along with his followers, from heaven to earth. There rebellion would be allowed to "have its full sway." The rebellious angels must be allowed "their day in court," or there would never be peace in heaven again. But what a price there would be to pay.

Is this account of rebellion in heaven imaginative? Far from it. The details are, but the facts are not. There are at least four passages in the Bible that support this idea of rebellion in heaven and the origin of evil in the world. In addition there are other ancient writings that bear this out (Apocrypha, etc.).

A passage in the Book of Revelation spells out this rebellion in the clearest of terms:

And there was war in heaven: Michael and his angels fought against the dragon; and the dragon fought and his angels, And prevailed not; neither was their place found any more in heaven. And the great dragon was cast out, that old serpent, called the Devil, and Satan, which deceiveth the whole world: he was cast out into the earth, and his angels were cast out with him (Rev. 12:7-9).

Also, there is a prophetic passage in the Book of Isaiah directed toward the king of Babylon. In his pride, the king is compared to the leader of this heavenly conflict. The passage is in the form of Hebrew poetry and is symbolic, but the symbolism is of the fallen angel. The passage not only compares the king to the rebellious archangel, but it prophesies the defeat of both.

How art thou fallen from heaven, O Lucifer, son of the morning! how art thou cut down to the ground, which didst weaken the nations! For thou hast said in thine heart, I will ascend into heaven, I will exalt my throne above the stars of God: I will sit also upon the mount of the congregation, in the sides of the north: I will ascend above the heights of the clouds; I will be like the most High. Yet thou shalt be brought down to hell, to the sides of the pit. They that see thee shall narrowly look upon thee, and consider thee, saying, Is this the man that made the earth tremble, that did shake kingdoms, That made the world as a wilderness, and destroyed the cities thereof; that opened not the house of his prisoners? (Isa. 14:12-17).

Ezekiel delivered a similar prophecy against another king, the king of Tyre. Like Isaiah, he too compared the king to the fallen archangel and prophesied defeat. Here the emphasis is more on the beauty of this rebellious one.

Thou hast been in Eden the garden of God; every precious stone was thy covering, the sardius, topaz, and the diamond, the beryl, the onyx, and the jasper, the sapphire, the emerald, and the carbuncle, and gold: the workman-ship of thy tabrets and of thy pipes was prepared in thee in the day that thou wast created. Thou art the anointed cherub that covereth; and I have set thee so: thou wast upon the holy mountain of God; thou hast walked up and down in the midst of the stones of fire. Thou wast perfect in thy ways from the day that thou wast created, till iniquity was found in thee. By the multitude of thy merchandise they have filled the midst of thee with violence, and thou hast sinned: therefore I will cast thee as profane out of the mountain of God: And I will destroy thee, O covering cherub, from the midst of the stones of fire. Thine heart was lifted up because of thy beauty, thou hast corrupted thy wisdom by reason of thy brightness: I will cast thee to the ground, I will lay thee before kings, that they may behold thee. Thou hast defiled thy sanctuaries by the multitude of thine iniquities, by the iniquity of thy traffic; therefore will I bring forth a fire from the midst of thee, it shall devour thee, and I will bring thee to ashes upon the earth in the sight of all them that behold thee. All they that know thee among the people shall be astonished at thee: Thou shalt be a terror, and never shalt thou be any more (Ezek. 28:13-19).

Also in Luke 10:18, Jesus sent seventy of his followers on a preaching and healing mission. They returned with the surprising news that even the devils were subject to them through his name. Unastonished, Jesus replied, "I beheld Satan as lightning fall from heaven." In answering his disciples, Jesus may have been referring to their present victory over Satan, but his reference may also have been to the rebellion that took place in heaven.

After this rebellion in heaven, God began "a long uphill climb" to prove his right to rule by love. His journey would one day take him up the hill of Calvary, and there would be a cross and suffering and death before victory would finally be won. But God would vindicate his holy name, and at the same time he would expose rebellion for the awful sin that it is.

By the evil action of his followers, Satan killed the Son of God. He thought the cross was his gain and God's loss. But Jesus overcame death through the resurrection and the cross became Satan's defeat and God's victory. Jesus' death reveals once and for all the completeness of Satan's rebellion and the fullness of God's love.

When this great drama of the ages ends, it will reveal through all eternity that God rules by love. The Son of God, with nail-scarred hands and feet and pierced side,[8] will be an eternal reminder of God's love and the price of rebellion. It will show what God was willing to suffer to demonstrate his love. Rebellion will be exposed; God's love will be revealed. There will never be rebellion in heaven again.

How will this great drama end? This battle between Satan and God, good and evil?

One day God will cry, "Stop." The final curtain will fall. There will be permanent and complete defeat for Satan and his followers. (Satan's followers include all who rebel against God's authority and his right to rule in their lives by love. They are the ones who reject God's forgiveness, and will not return to him by way of the cross. They are those who would rather be ruled by self in hell than be ruled by God in heaven.) Jesus shall return. God's judgment will be upon the world and Satan and upon all those whose reply to God is *"My will be done,"* instead of *"Thy will be done."* At the moment when God brings down the curtain, sin will have broken its last heart. Rebellion will have had its "day in court." The cup of human suffering will have been drained of its last bitter drop.

"And God shall wipe away all tears from their eyes; and there shall be no more death, neither sorrow, nor crying, neither shall there be any more pain: for the former things are passed away" (Rev. 21:4).

3

God Doesn't Lead a Sheltered Life

Father Joseph Damien was a Belgium missionary serving in Honolulu, Hawaii. Upon learning of a leper colony on the island of Molokai, he obtained permission and went to live among the six-hundred unfortunate outcasts.[1]

He encouraged the lepers to build better homes for themselves along with a water line to a spring, a mile away from where they carried water. On the sheltered side of the peninsula, protected from the elements, they built a small primitive hospital.

Though Father Damien was able to improve their physical lot, his effort to meet their spiritual needs met with little success. He often felt like an outcast himself among those in the colony; he confessed to dreadful loneliness and separation from the people—for you see, he was the only healthy man on an island made up entirely of lepers.

But one morning while preparing breakfast, something unusual happened. While Father Damien was pouring boiling water into a pan, some of it splashed onto his bare foot. He did not feel the pain. . . . It was boiling water, and he did not feel the pain? He looked in astonishment at his foot, then the truth broke through: One of the first signs of leprosy is immunity to pain. He was now a leper himself! Despite the shock of his discovery, he was overcome with a strange feeling of joy. He immediately rang the bell, summoning his poor flock to church. He leaped into his pulpit, looked at his congregation, then opening his arms wide, as though to embrace them, he smiled and said, "Fellow lepers, fellow lepers."[2]

From that day on, Father Damien's spiritual ministry to the needs of the lepers was well rewarded. Many turned in faith to the Lord. And in their newfound faith, the lepers discovered a new courage to see them through this life and a wonderful hope for the next.

What changed their attitude? Simply this: They knew that in his love, Father Damien had given himself for them. They saw Christ's love demonstrated in his life as Father Damien became a part of their own suffering.

I thought, as I heard that story for the first time, *this is exactly what God did.* In Jesus he deliberately identified with a suffering world. And he identified with it through his own suffering.

Although God was not responsible for mankind's suffering, he could share in that suffering. He could not rid the world of suffering—at least not just now—but he could let people know that he was suffering with them. And he would show all of them! So God became a man and suffered and died on a cross. True, the cross is more than this, but this is part of it.

George MacDonald wrote in "Unspoken Sermon," "The Son of God suffered unto death, not that men might not suffer, but that their sufferings might be like his."

One day a scientist was watching some ants in the yard of his home. He marveled at their industrious energy, but he detected a weakness in their intelligence.

He had placed a bit of food on the top of a table some distance from an ant nest, where it was soon discovered by the scouts. As the ants began carrying the food back to their nest he moved it closer; but they persisted in traveling the old route around the edge of the table, a familiar but longer distance. The scientist kept moving the food closer, but even when it was almost at the nest the ants continued to follow the older route instead of the shorter way. He built obstacles along their trail, hoping to divert the ants and force them to take the shortcut. But they continued to travel their old, familiar route back and forth to get the food.

I wish I could tell them, he thought. *If I could become an ant, I could explain it to them.* Then he reflected, *No, if I became an ant I would simply act and think like an ant. I would have to become both an ant and a man.*

This is exactly the situation that God faced when he came to earth as Jesus Christ. He would have to be both man and God. He would be

God, but at the same time have the limitations of man. This is what the incarnation is all about. In some mysterious way God did become man, the man Jesus. "God was in Christ, reconciling the world unto himself" (2 Cor. 5:19).

Somehow, in some way, God had to tell people he loved them. But he had to do it more than by just saying it. He had to explain it in a way that they would understand.

What better way to tell them of his concern than to demonstrate his love? And what better way to demonstrate that love than go all the way, even from birth to death? God would become a part of man's life; he too, would suffer and die. By this he could say, "I want you to know I understand your suffering, I am with you in this all the way. I may be your Creator, but I am not above your suffering."

I read an unusual and imaginative story one day that illustrates this identifying of God with human beings.

The great judgment morning had arrived. It was the end of the age. The nations were gathered together, and billions of people were scattered across a great plain before the judgment throne of God. For some it was a time of victory; they had lived, and died, for this hour. For others it was a day of defeat; they sat in humility, with heads bowed in shame.

But some near the front were standing arrogantly with an attitude of defiance. A few in the group even shook their fists in the direction of the throne.

"God won't judge me," cried one.

"No," shouted others.

"How can he?" Came still another voice. "How can God have the nerve?"

"Yes," echoed an olive-skinned brunette, jerking up a sleeve to reveal a tattooed number from a concentration camp. She was a Jewish girl and had died a horrible death. "We have endured terror, beating, torture, and death," she shouted. "What does God know about such things?"

In another group, a black man lowered his collar to show an ugly rope burn. "What about this?" he demanded. "I got into trouble and was lynched because I was black. We suffered suffocation on slave ships; were wrenched from the arms of loved ones; toiled in the fields until death alone gave us release. What does God know about that kind of a life?"

Far out across the plains, from every generation, there was the thunder of thousands of voices from hundreds of groups, each with a complaint against God.

Their grievance was against a God who lived far away up in heaven: where all was sweetness and light; where he had his angels to serve him day and night; where there was no weeping, no fear, no hunger, no hatred—only love. What did God know about suffering?

"Indeed," they all agreed, "what does he know about life, life down there? Or what does he know about death and pain, and suffering?"

"After all," they said, "God leads a pretty sheltered life."

Hearing the protests, God invited each group to send out a leader, and he would hear their case. So they gathered in the center of the great plain to consult with each other. Finally, they drew up a list of their conditions.

If God were to judge them, they contended, there were some things he had to do. Before God would be qualified to be their judge, he had to know something about life down there; and they pointed in the direction of earth. The overwhelming demand was that he be sent to earth—not as God but as man—and not as any man, but as one who would live under the conditions they had mutually agreed upon.

The list of conditions was ready. As each leader announced his portion of the terms of the sentence, loud shouts of approval went up from the great throng.

First, they would limit him so that he could not use his divine power to help himself in any way. If he got thirsty, or hungry, or tired, he had to find his own water, food, or rest just like everyone else.

Next, he was to be born a Jew. Everyone agreed to that, since, of all peoples, the Jews seemed to have suffered the most.

To make it more difficult for him, the question of his legitimacy was to be questioned. What a shadow this will cast over him. Few would know his real father. That will give him a stigma he would find hard to overcome.

"Let him live in poverty. That will teach him some of the facts of life. Let him depend upon others for most of his living, not knowing where the next meal will come from. Let him know hunger, cold, unfriendliness, and loneliness.

"Then, let him champion a cause that will be unpopular and opposed by many. In his zeal to advance his cause let him cut across every minor tradition, social custom, and prejudice of men and religious leaders. Let him be labeled a radical, a dreamer.

"In the midst of all of this let him try to describe in limited words what no man has ever experienced with his five senses. Let him try to communicate himself as God, that will throw him! It will be like trying to tell a blind man what a red sunset is like. Or telling a man who has never tasted grape jelly how grape jelly tastes. Let him know the frustrations of having people misunderstand things he understands all too clearly.

"Let him be indicted on false charges by false testimony. Let his great deeds be criticized as bad; his right acts as wrong; his good as evil. This will surely destroy him.

"Then let him be tried before a prejudiced jury and a cowardly judge so that everything he says will be twisted and used against him. He will learn about prejudice from that.

"Allow him to be abandoned, alone, and completely separated from friends and loved ones. Talk about loneliness and suffering!

"Then let him be tortured and killed in a most shameful and embarrassing way. Execute him as a common criminal. What's more, let him die a painful death in the company of criminals."

When the last one had finished his announcement of the conditions under which God was to be tested on earth, there was silence. No one uttered a word. No one moved. A great hush fell over the entire plain. For suddenly everyone knew, God had already served his sentence.

It was God they crucified: the incarnate God, the Son of God, Jesus Christ. The carpenter of Nazareth *was* the Creator of the world, and God was suffering with him.

An artist has tried to capture this unique oneness of God with his Son in a painting that hangs in one of our nation's art galleries. It is a picture of Jesus hanging on the cross. When one first looks at the painting, there appears to be nothing but dense darkness in the background. All one sees is the figure of Jesus on the cross. But as one looks behind the scene another figure gradually emerges from the darkness. It is the form of God; with hands outstretched, he is supporting Jesus. The agony on the Father's face is even more striking than that on the face of the Son.

In some mysterious way, beyond human understanding, that which happened to Jesus also happened to God. And as with Jesus, that which happens to us also touches God. Just as a cup of water is a part of the ocean, so our suffering becomes a part of God's suffering.

God is like a loving father who pulls a sobbing, hurt child close as though trying to take all the pain unto himself. He does not take it all away, but he suffers with us and assures us that he cares and knows our grief and pain by identifying with our suffering.

I heard a story that illustrated God's presence in our suffering in this way. Briefly it was this: A father had just received word his son had been killed in the war; he rushed into his pastor's study. In desperation he cried out, "Where was God; where was God when my son died?"

In a moment of divine insight the pastor calmly answered the distraught father: "God was just where he was when his own Son died on a hillside outside Jerusalem."

I am confident the apostle Peter knew this care and concern of God from personal experience when he wrote: "Humble yourselves therefore under the mighty hand of God, that he may exalt you in due time: Casting all your care upon him; for he careth for you" (1 Pet. 5:6-7).

There is a very impressive promise in the Book of Isaiah concerning God's care and assurance that he will be present with us in all situations. Though written in poetic fashion, and to the nation of Israel, nevertheless it is a promise that can be claimed by us as individuals. "When thou passest through the waters, I will be with thee; and through the rivers, they shall not overflow thee: when thou walkest through the fire, thou shalt not be burned; neither shall the flame kindle upon thee" (Isa. 43:2).

David expressed this same assurance when he wrote the twenty-third Psalm: "Yea, though I walk through the valley of the shadow of death, I will fear no evil: for thou art with me" (v. 4). Have you noticed the word *through*? Not just "into" the valley of the shadow of death, but into and out again on the other side. Whether David was thinking about an actual valley or speaking figuratively about death is not clear, but in either case, the Lord is with us as we face both the rigors of life and the reality of death.

Our Lord promised he would be with us, but he never promised that life would be easy and free from suffering. In fact, as we read the Gospels, Jesus seemed to go out of his way to remind us that we will not be able to claim immunity to trouble by following him. On one occasion he said, "In the world ye shall have tribulation: but be of good cheer; I have overcome the world" (John 16:33). At another time he reminded his disciples: "Remember the word that I said unto you, The servant is not greater than his lord. If they have persecuted me, they will also persecute you; if they have kept my saying, they will keep yours also" (John 15:20).

In a sense Jesus was saying that we may get into more trouble by following him than by trying to remain neutral and not getting involved. However, he promised those of us who cast their lot with him that he will be with us and see us through.

Annie Johnson Flint has expressed these promises beautifully in her poem "What God Hath Promised":

> God hath not promised skies always blue,
> Flower-strewn pathways all our lives through;
> God hath not promised sun without rain,
> Joy without sorrow, peace without pain.
>
> God hath not promised we shall not know
> Toil and temptation, trouble and woe;
> He hath not told us we shall not bear
> Many a burden, many a care.
>
> God hath not promised smooth roads and wide,
> Swift, easy travel, needing no guide;
> Never a mountain, rocky and steep,
> Never a river turgid and deep.
>
> But God hath promised strength for the day,
> Rest for the labor, light for the way,
> Grace for the trials, help from above,
> Unfailing sympathy, undying love.

Someone has said: "Walk with God in the sunshine, and he will walk with you in the shadows. Be with him on the mountains, and he will be with you in the valleys." The following story illustrates this point.

Jim did not know much according to worldly standards. But he knew enough to realize his need for the Savior. One night in a small church in the city, he surrendered his life to Christ as Lord and Master.

Jim was so grateful for his newly found friendship with Christ that each day during the noon hour he hurriedly walked back to the church for a moment to pray.

One day the pastor said to him: "I see you come in every day, out of breath; you kneel for a few moments at the altar, then you are up and on your way again. Why?"

"Sir," he explained, "I have thirty minutes for lunch. I can walk to the church in about fifteen minutes and back in the same time. That gives me just a few moments for prayer. I love the Lord, so I just kneel here and say, "Hello, Jesus, this is Jim.' "

A few days later, Jim stepped out in front of a moving auto. He was rushed to the hospital and placed in a cast from head to toe. As the days passed, Jim became a real inspiration to everyone around him. Despite his pain he soon became known as the most cheerful patient in the ward.

One day the nurse asked, "Jim, how can you be such a comfort and joy to everyone when you would seem to be the one that needs cheering up?"

"Every day," he said, "I have this friend that comes in and speaks to me."

The nurse smiled in sympathy. She knew he had not had a visitor or even received a card since being there. "Jim," she said, "no one comes to see you. You don't have any visitors. You don't even have a family."

"Oh, but I do have a visitor," replied Jim. "Every day, just about noon, he comes in . . . just for a moment. He always says, 'Hello Jim, this is Jesus.' "

Walk with him in the bright days, and he will walk with you in the rain.

Clark Poling was one of the four chaplains that gave up his life jacket and drowned when the *S.S. Dorchester* was sunk during World War II. His father, Dr. Daniel Poling, tells this story about Clark when he was a young boy.

When Clark was only a small boy, he faced a very serious operation on his throat. He protested for a number of days, but the condition grew worse. Finally the operation had to be done.

Despite his objection, Clark was soon on his way to the operating room. His last words before he went under the anesthetic were, "Dad, will you stay with me?"

"Of course," was the quick reply.

But after the boy was unconscious, Dr. Poling said he was tempted to leave. There was really nothing he could do. Then he remembered the boy's pathetic plea and his own promise, so he stayed by the operating table.

When his son opened his eyes, his first words to his father were, "Dad, did you stay?"

Dr. Poling was able to reply, "Yes, I stayed." He was always glad he had.

"And when Clark went down along with the other chaplains," said Dr. Poling, "I am sure he asked the same question: 'Father, will you stay with me?'"

"I know Clark heard again that same answer, only this time from his Heavenly Father: 'Yes, Clark, I'll stay. I will be with you all the way.'"

Didn't Jesus say that a sparrow does not fall to the ground without our Father's knowledge? And he also said we are more valuable than many sparrows (Matt. 10:29-31).

Of course Jesus knows us, and he cares.

> O yes, He cares, I know He cares,
> His heart is touched with my grief;
> When the days are weary, The long nights dreary,
> I know my Savior cares.

> —Frank E. Graeff

Yes, he cares; God doesn't lead a sheltered life.

4

Pound for Pound?

Is suffering a direct result of sin? Many think so. If so, is it measured out to us "pound for pound": a pound of suffering for a pound of sin? Is it an "eye for an eye" or a "tooth for a tooth" kind of punishment? Is our goodness rewarded with an equal amount of blessing, and are we punished for our sins with a proportionate amount of suffering?

Regardless of all evidence to the contrary, many still believe this simple "pound for pound" formula explains most suffering. The real tragedy is when this kind of an answer is used to explain to someone else the reason for their suffering. Well-wishing friends (friends?) proposing this idea only add to the suffering, causing a feeling of guilt as they attempt to "comfort" those going through a trying experience.

In the Old Testament, Job, a righteous man, was forced to suffer the buffeting of Satan. His friends came to encourage him and give him advice. They were from this "cause-effect" school and were sure they had the right answer: his misery was due entirely to sin. If he would only repent, he could reverse the tide of his suffering.

Job refused to "fit their mold." In essence he said, "I know I am not perfect, but I also know I haven't sinned enough to cause this." In fact, he was so sure of his ground that he called upon God and began to argue the point. Job was confident that his "comforters" were wrong. He was sure their "pound for pound" philosophy broke down in his case. And it did. Job was right!

His suffering was not at all related to his sin. In fact, it was just the opposite. His suffering resulted from his righteousness. Job was such a good man that Satan accused him of being good because of the good things he received from God. Then God said, "Go ahead, test him, and see."

In the end Job was vindicated. God honored him before his friends and showed them they were wrong in their thinking.

In the comic strip "Peanuts," Charles Schultz illustrates this point by a conversation between Lucy and Snoopy.

Lucy is scolding Snoopy and says, "You know why your doghouse burned down? Because you sinned, that's why! You're being punished for something you did wrong! That is the way these things always work!"

Snoopy, with tongue extended in the direction of Lucy, answers simply, "Bleah!"

Then in a quiet reflective pose, he gazes away and says, "Her kind deserve to be bleahed!"

And those kind do deserve to be "bleahed." Their thinking is wrong. Sin does cause suffering, but suffering is not always a result of sin.

Jesus had difficulty in dealing with this kind of thinking among the people of his time. Like many today they believed good people prospered, and evil people suffered. They thought one could measure the degree of a person's sin by the way that person suffered and calculate goodness by the way a person was blessed.

The story of the blind man, found in the ninth chapter of the Gospel of John, reflects this thinking. Even though the "pound for pound" theory of suffering was not the main issue, Jesus would not let the theory go unchallenged. He denied it categorically and attempted to correct the false idea.

In the story, Jesus was walking along with his disciples. Seeing a man who had been blind since birth, the disciples were curious. They asked, "Master, who did sin, this man, or his parents, that he was born blind?" (v. 2).

Jesus' answer was emphatic. "Neither," he said.

It was not because the man had sinned, nor his parents, that he was born blind. Rather, it was that the work of God might be shown. Then Jesus healed him.

What is the conclusion to be drawn from Jesus' answer? Just this. God doesn't "go around" deliberately blinding unborn children as a way of punishing their parents. And, of course, neither does he willfully afflict innocent children, who have not sinned. Birth defects, even blindness, are not God's punishment on a mother or father, or a child, because of sin.

However, such things as venereal disease can, and sometimes do, cause blindness in children. And it may well be that the sin of adultery resulted in the parents having the disease. But here again God is not punishing the parents or child, even though the sin of the mother or father may have indirectly caused the blindness.

Many things have a bearing on the well-being of an unborn child. And one's ignorance of the consequences does not prevent the harmful effects. A mother can harm her unborn child by the use of alcohol, cigarettes, even poor nutrition, or certain drugs, either illegal or prescribed. But God is not to blame.

The story of the drug thalidomide is a good example. Mothers who took this apparently innocent tranquilizer harmed their unborn children. Hundreds of newborn babies were affected before the cause could be found.

German measles can have a heartbreaking effect on unborn children. Here is an example where neither sin nor ignorance can be blamed. Usually the mother is accidentally exposed to the disease at a very critical time—often before she knows she is pregnant. She contracts the disease, and the damage is done. (However, a vaccine is available today.)

Many mothers and fathers suffer from untold guilt because they believe God is "getting back at them" by punishing their sins through a deformed child. "Not so," says Jesus. However, as he pointed out, in the case of the blind man, God may use suffering in order that his name might be honored.

Fanny J. Crosby is an excellent example of how one's suffering can bring glory to God. Many beautiful songs that honor the name of Jesus have been written by her. These songs might never have been composed had she not suffered blindness as a young child. Because of her daughter's blindness, Miss Crosby's mother challenged her to write poetry. Other successful blind poets became her examples and gave her courage. This courage was expressed by her, even at the young age of eight, in her poem "Blind But Happy."

O what a happy soul am I!
Although I cannot see,

I am resolved that in this world
Contented I will be;
How many blessings I enjoy
That other people don't!
To weep and sigh because I'm blind,
I cannot, and I won't.

As though wanting to cover the entire matter of the "sin-suffering" theory, Jesus gave two other, but different, examples. In both illustrations, Jesus refuted the idea that so much sin equaled so much punishment.

In the Gospel of Luke the subject of suffering became the topic of conversation between Jesus and some of his listeners. Here is the account.

There were present at that season some that told him of the Galilaeans, whose blood Pilate had mingled with their sacrifices. And Jesus answering said unto them, Suppose ye that these Galilaeans were sinners above all the Galilaeans, because they suffered such things? I tell you, Nay: but, except ye repent, ye shall all likewise perish.

Or those eighteen, upon whom the tower in Siloam fell, and slew them, think ye that they were sinners above all men that dwelt in Jerusalem? I tell you, Nay: but, except ye repent, ye shall all likewise perish (13:1-5).

(In his warnings, Jesus was probably referring to that which was going to happen to Jerusalem soon. It occurred in AD 70 when the Roman general Titus destroyed the city.)

Some men from Galilee had been murdered by the order of Pilate, the Roman governor. The event happened at the Temple area while these worshiping Galileans were preparing their animals for sacrifice. Some of the murdered men's blood actually splashed on the sacrificial animals.

There was a lot of discussion about this strange event. How could these men, who, at that very time, were offering sacrifices, have been such terrible sinners? Yet, somehow they must have been great sinners to deserve such a fate.

Jesus again said, "No! They were sinners, but no worse than others," implying that the men's relationship to God and the circumstances of their death were not connected.

The other account concerned a tower which fell on eighteen men, probably workmen, at the famous pool of Siloam. (This was the same pool where the blind man, mentioned earlier, was healed.)

The tower may have fallen because of poor construction, shifting of the foundation, or perhaps an earthquake (sometimes wrongly called an "act of God"). Probably the tragedy occurred during the building of an aqueduct. Because Temple money was being used by the Romans for the project, this was considered to be an affront to God. And God could be expected to demonstrate his wrath; anything that happened was more than deserved. Regardless of why the tower fell, the conclusion was that the men who died were greater sinners than the average—a pound of suffering for a pound of sin!

Jesus said, "No!" Again implying that regardless of the spiritual condition of these eighteen men suffering cannot be traced directly back to punishment for sin.

Natural calamities (the tower) or birth defects (one born blind) cannot be attributed directly to sin. However, this in no way rules out suffering that often does come because of people's sin. Towers do fall on people because of poor and cheap construction by contractors; such remiss is a sin. Babies are born blind because a mother may have contracted syphilis through adultery. People do suffer murder as a direct result of sin in the heart of a murderer. But God is not personally taking vengeance upon the sufferer.

From my boyhood I remember a vivid example of indirect suffering because of sin. I am sure the story could be multiplied a thousand times.

During the depression days, my father owned a small grocery store, and often furnished credit to the farmers in the area. Many times he would provide them groceries for almost a full year with the only hope for payment being in the fall, when the "crops were in."

One spring, a new man moved into the community and asked my father for credit. As with other creditors, my father agreed to supply groceries for him and his family until harvesttime.

When fall came, the farmer made more than enough to pay his debts. But he refused to pay my father. Instead, he took the money and bought a team of fine horses for his farm. My father approached him about his grocery bill; he appealed to his sense of honesty, but the farmer insisted he would keep the horses and refused to pay.

One Saturday, late at night, the farmer was returning home with the horses from a nearby town, riding one of them. They were rather spirited animals, and the lights of an approaching car "spooked" them. Bolting, they threw the man to the ground. In the excitement he was trampled and died.

For days, as a small boy, I wondered about the tragedy. My reasoning went like this: "If that man had paid my father, he wouldn't have had the extra money. Without the extra money he wouldn't have bought the horses. If he hadn't bought the horses, he wouldn't have been on the road. And if he hadn't been on the road, he wouldn't have been killed that tragic Saturday night."

It all sounded so reasonable to my young mind. And, you know, it still does. Perhaps here is a lesson on the consequences of sin. Suffering is not always caused by sin, but sin can cause suffering. Wrong acts seem to have a way of catching up with us. "The mills of the gods grind slowly, but they grind exceedingly fine." "Chickens do come home to roost." But it is not a "pound for pound" kind of punishment at the hand of God.

So then we should do good. Then if we suffer, we will not consider it punishment for our sins. There is a Scripture that says: "For what glory is it, if, when ye be buffeted for your faults, ye shall take it patiently? but if, when ye do well, and suffer for it, ye take it patiently, this is acceptable with God" (1 Pet. 2:20).

One morning when I was in seminary class, the professor came in late. He explained the reason for his delay by telling the following story:

He was on his way to class when he stopped to pick up a well-dressed businessman sitting on the curb next to his car which was out of gas. He was visibly disturbed and soon began to pour out his troubles.

The man said he had just received word that his only son had been killed in Korea. He began to weep bitterly and confessed through sobs that for months he had been unfaithful to his wife. He was sure that God was punishing him for his sins by taking his son.

The professor concluded the story with this comment: "I do not know that God was punishing this man by taking his son, but I do know that this man was being punished, nevertheless."

I remember a very successful young businessman who was married and had a fine family. In his business he was required to raise large amounts of money through personal contact with people. An elderly lady, prominent in the community, was to make a large contribution toward his work. One morning she was found murdered in her home. The neighbors knew the young man often visited her. In fact, he was the last one seen with her before her death.

He was a suspect! The police checked with his wife. She admitted he had not come home the evening of the murder. So he was arrested and charged with murder.

The young man was not guilty, but in order to establish an alibi he had to confess to a secret affair with another woman and that he had spent the night with her. She verified his statement, and charges were dropped. He had established his innocence of murder, but only at the expense of having to confess his guilt of adultery.

"Be sure your sin will find you out" (Num. 32:23). Sin has a way of always "tripping us up"—if not in this life, perhaps in the next. "Be not deceived; God is not mocked: for whatsoever a man soweth, that shall he also reap" (Gal. 6:7). This principle is well illustrated and documented in the Bible. One example is Jacob, whose name means "one who takes by trickery." He was a real confidence man who literally lived up to his name. Look at his life.

Though he was not born first, he tricked his twin brother, Esau, out of the inheritance which always belonged to the firstborn. In order to save his life, he had to leave home. Soon he met his match in Laban, an uncle who was to become his father-in-law. Jacob was tricked by Laban concerning his bride. As a result, he had to work fourteen years for the woman he loved. Jacob then retaliated by a crafty maneuver against Laban that provided him with a large number of Laban's livestock.

Jacob's life seemed to be one continuous experience of tricking and being tricked. Later, Jacob's own sons tricked him concerning his son Joseph: They sold Joseph into slavery and tricked Jacob into believing that a wild beast had killed him. It was not until Joseph showed a spirit of forgiveness toward his brothers that the chain of deceit was finally broken.

Suffering may not be a "pound for pound" type of punishment of sin, but sin seems to eventually bring about its own suffering. God doesn't always have payday on "Saturday night," nor does he settle his accounts "in the fall of the year." But God always has what Dr. R. G. Lee called "Payday Someday."

5

Attention!

When the Army drill sergeant barks, "Atten . . . chut!" he means more than, "Would you please give me your attention." *Attention!* is a one-word command. It means, "Face straight ahead, arms at side, eyes forward." That is an order! You are to be ready and alert for the next command.

The following is an old story that illustrates the direction of this chapter better than anything I can think of. You have probably heard some variation of it many times.

The setting is a rural farm area in one of our southern states. Before the present era of a tractor on every plot, the farmer used the mule to work the farm—a valuable animal.

Now, mules have never been known for their spirit of cooperation; in fact, they can be downright stubborn. But this farmer had a mule that was even more obstinate than the average.

One Saturday morning, at the town square, a stranger was boasting of his ability to break mules. He vowed that there was not a mule alive that he couldn't train.

Challenging his ability, the farmer invited the stranger out to his farm to meet his old stubborn mule.

Early Monday morning, the stranger was there ready to begin his work. The farmer pointed out the mule and stepped back beside the barn to watch the performance. Slowly, the stranger approached the animal. The mule looked surprised and alarmed. For a full minute the two gazed into each other's eyes. Then stepping back and picking up a length of a two-by-four, the stranger swung the beam with both hands. It came crashing down squarely on the mule's head right between his eyes.

The mule reeled back, sank to the ground, and shook his head. In a few minutes he staggered to his feet and fixed a glassy stare of unbelief on the stranger. Again, with a mighty swing, the trainer let fly with the two-by-four. For the second time the mule sank to the ground, dazed.

By this time, the farmer had stepped forward. "Look, mister," he said, "I hired you to come out here to train my mule, not to kill him."

"Well," drawled the stranger, "I can see you sure don't know much about training mules. The first thing you have to do is to get their attention."

A person in his response to God can be about as stubborn as a mule. Sometimes God has to get his attention. Sometimes God has to allow him to be "knocked down" before he will stop long enough to listen. Some suffering is like that; God is only trying to attract our attention.

In visiting the hospital, I have heard patients say, "Pastor, I guess God had to put me on my back to get me to look up; he had to put me in the hospital in order for me to listen." So sometimes God allows our suffering for this reason: to get our attention.

On long drives over stretches of superhighways, our senses often become dull. After miles of smooth, straight roads, we become listless and careless toward things about us. Driving like this can be dangerous.

I have driven along a highway many times, half asleep, when suddenly I was startled and made wide-awake by a noisy rumbling. It was a vibration that could be heard and felt throughout the car. What had happened to the car? Nothing! It was the highway. A stretch of the roadway had been deliberately made rough. It was a warning signal before approaching a caution area. Small grooves or ridges had been formed at right angles across the road. They were there for this purpose: to alert drowsy drivers. Such roughness is not dangerous or even uncomfortable, but it is enough to disturb one and to make him alert.

In California, as in many other states, billions of small, raised, circular discs have been cemented along the center divider lines of many highways. (Called "Bott's Dots," these little discs are named after the man who invented them.) Like the roughened stretch of highway, they alert a driver when he drifts out of his lane.

God has arranged our lives like this. Along the "highway" we call life, he has allowed certain disturbances to alert us. They are not meant to be roadblocks to stop us, but only small irritants to disturb us. God uses them to wake us up, to get our attention. When things are going smoothly, we tend to forget God. Sometimes we have to be reminded that he is still in control. I am afraid that most of us take too many things for granted: our health, our family, our friends, even life itself. Worst of all, we even take God for granted.

The old country preacher was probably right when he used the phrase *status quo* a number of times in his morning sermon. After the service, he was approached by one of his members who asked the meaning of the word.

Hesitating, he groped for an answer. Finally the preacher responded: "Why, my friend, status quo is Latin for the rut we are in."

The status quo may be comfortable, but it is not the best way to live our lives. When life goes along the same way day after day, we grow dull, careless, and unappreciative. Someone has said a rut traveled long soon becomes comfortable, and a rut becomes a grave with both ends knocked out.

It has been said, rather facetiously, that God cannot make a valley without mountains. I suppose, by the definition of the words, this is true. Valleys are formed where mountains meet. One depends upon the other. Perhaps it is just as true that we cannot have a mountaintop experience without a valley experience. One needs the other for contrast. We cannot fully appreciate one without comparing it to the other.

A man on a bus was complaining about his tight shoes. His feet were killing him.

"Why do you wear tight shoes if they hurt your feet?" asked another rider.

"Because it feels so good when I get home and take them off," was the reply.

There may be more truth than humor in his answer. The comparison makes the difference.

The little kindergarten girl wanted to use the white paint for her picture, but she wanted to use it on white paper. Finally the teacher gave her dark paper. Then she understood: white colors were for dark paper, dark colors were for white paper. It is the difference that made the picture.

Look at a black-and-white photograph. It takes the various tones of gray, and the blacks and whites—the contrast, to make the picture.

In a symphony it is the various sounds of the instruments that give quality to the music. The bass sounds are needed as well as the treble sounds. One without the other would be monotonous and boring. Variety in the notes adds to the beauty.

The old mountaineer's wife tried to explain this principle to her husband. He had ordered a bass fiddle from the mail-order catalog. Night after night, "thump, thump, thump," he slapped the strings, while grasping the neck of the instrument solidly with his other hand.

Finally his wife could stand the noise no longer.

"Paw," she said in her best diplomatic way, "I notice the fellows on television don't hold their hand in one place on the neck. They go up and down."

"I know, Maw," he said, "but those fellows are looking; I've found the place."

Despite the logic of the argument, it's the diversity of notes that makes the music.

In his book *The Problem of Pain* C. S. Lewis says:

God whispers to us in our pleasure, speaks in our conscience, but shouts in our pains: It is His megaphone to rouse a deaf world. . . .
We have all noticed how hard it is to turn our thoughts to God when everything is going well. We find God an interruption. When we "have all we want" it is sad when "all" does not include God. As St. Augustine wrote, "God wants to give us something, but cannot, because our hands are full, there's nowhere for Him to put it."[1]

One day as I was writing an article on suffering, I stopped for a few minutes to discuss the idea with my daughter, Kathleen. I suggested that suffering through disappointments and problems are sometimes God's way of drawing us near to him, to attract our attention. I asked her opinion.

She stopped her studying, closed her book, and looked up slowly. Her response surprised me. It was as though she had been looking for an answer and suddenly found it. She said, rather reflectively, "Sure, that's it."

Then she explained. "You know," she said, "when I am having trouble (and she described a recent problem she was facing with her class scheduling), I always turn to the Lord. I'm closer then, I pray a lot more. Maybe he is telling me I should be closer to him all the time and not just when I have a problem."

It's no trite statement that declares, "When life knocks you to your knees, you are in a good position to pray."

Even though God allows suffering to enter our lives in order to attract our attention, it does not follow that suffering will always draw us nearer to him. Sometimes the results will be just the opposite. There is a chance that suffering will drive us farther away from God, and our response can drive a wedge between us and God.

Many great losses come into our lives. However, we lose the most when our faith is affected because of suffering. When our faith is affected, the suffering has not been diminished. Without a strong faith, suffering becomes a double tragedy, for we have lost our source of strength for overcoming the suffering. As we retreat into the darkness of doubt and disbelief, we do not allow God to speak to us through our suffering. Therefore, our loss is compounded.

Suffering tests the quality of our faith. Jesus told the story of two men who built their houses on different foundations (Matt. 7:24-27). One built on the solid rock, the other on shifting sand. When trouble came, it came from three directions: the rains came down, the floods came up, and the wind blew against each house. Both suffered the same. The difference? The house built on the rock withstood the storm, the other did not.

The point of the story is clear. Trouble comes to all, but the one who builds his life on faith in Jesus Christ will stand. The life lived apart from Christ will "crumble" in the face of suffering.

> On Christ, the solid Rock, I stand;
> All other ground is sinking sand.[2]

In my ministry I have spoken to thousands of people who have faced suffering and pain. Invariably I have said something like this: "This is not good; suffering is never good in itself. God is not the author of it. He has allowed it to happen, but he did not send it. So let God draw you nearer to him through this experience. He has promised that he will bring good out of it if you will let him. But, if you allow this to drive you away from God, it will be a far greater tragedy than you are already facing."

During World War II, I spent some time in China. I came to realize that the Chinese have a deep insight into life. They have even written some of their philosophy into the very characters of their language. I was told that the symbol for "crisis" is made up of two characters. One is the word *opportunity*, and the other *danger* (or "disaster"). By combining the two, a crisis becomes both an opportunity and a danger.

Suffering is like that. It too can be a dangerous opportunity: either an opportunity to draw us nearer to God, or as a wedge to drive us farther away.

In his book *Victory Over Suffering*, A. Graham Ikin has a chapter entitled "Break Out, Break Down, or Break Through?"[3]

Although this is not exactly the way Mr. Ikin uses the idea, nevertheless, the three terms illustrate the three ways of meeting the crisis of suffering.

We may "break out." That is, we may try to break away from God and run. This becomes rebellion and results in bitterness. Here we find ourselves farther from him than we were in the beginning.

We may "break down." We succumb to the disaster of suffering. We surrender to it. We break under its pressure and accept it without finding either purpose or meaning. This condition is not as damaging as the first, but we are not better off for our experience.

Or we "break through." Our suffering becomes an opportunity to break through to God, and he breaks through to us. He gets our attention, and we get his blessings, if we give him the chance.

My oldest daughter, Janet, told me that it seems our suffering experiences could be compared to running the scale on a piano. We go through one full octave and the last note becomes the first note of the next higher octave. We either go on or drop back to begin the same octave over again. In a similar way, if we successfully move through a suffering experience we find ourselves on a higher plane. But if the experience makes us bitter, we drop back to the first octave and begin again.

Suffering, as nothing else, can quickly call attention to our insufficiency. Nothing drives us so rapidly to our knees or causes us to look up and seek higher ground.

A strange analogy of this truth is found among cattle on some South American plains. In the hot and humid season great herds of cattle become weak in the sultry lowlands. The animals would soon die if it were not for a strange balance found in nature. When it seems there is no hope, great swarms of stinging flies arrive and fiercely attack the poor beasts, adding to their misery. The animals flee in panic toward the hills. The insects continue to pursue the cattle higher and higher. One looks in sympathy at the bleeding, panting, and tormented herds. Yet, they have, by their very trouble, been driven to save their lives. For at the higher, cooler level the insects leave the herds, and once again they regain their health in a drier and milder climate.

God may work in much of our suffering in an attempt to bring us to "higher ground." He wants to attract us to himself. We may find that our loss of health, money, friends, position, or whatever problem may be used by God in such a way so as to accomplish in our lives what could not happen any other way.

My heart has no desire to stay
Where doubts arise and fears dismay;
Tho some may dwell where these abound,
My prayer, my aim is higher ground.[4]

6

God Is Not Finished with Me

Sometime ago I attended a weekend of meetings where many of the young people wore buttons with the letters *P B P G I N F W M Y* on them. I soon discovered that this was not some Greek word, or a motto in Swahili, but rather letters that stand for: "Please Be Patient, God Is Not Finished with Me Yet."

The motto expressed the idea that even though a person is a Christian, he is not perfect. He asks that others be patient and not judge the wearer too harshly for his immature actions. He is saying: "Remember, I am still a babe in Christ; I haven't arrived yet. I am still growing."

When I heard this explanation for the letters, I thought, *Suffering is like that.* God is working in our lives. He is working out certain things for our good and for his glory. It is a refining process to strengthen our faith and to develop our character.

God is busy molding, shaping, painting, carving—always working toward an end. True, we do not always know what the immediate goal is, or what he is trying to achieve, but one day it will be revealed. We may not even know in this life, for this is only "a part of the picture," but one day he will show us the completed work.

This is why it is unfair to judge God in light of a present situation of suffering. Just as it would be unfair to judge an artist by an unfinished painting, so it is unfair to judge God by his incomplete work.

Leslie D. Weatherhead, in his book *Why Do Men Suffer?* makes this comment about "snap judgment" concerning God and the problem of suffering.

When men cry out against, or deny the existence of, God because of human suffering—as they often do—I find comfort in the thought that I should be foolish to draw final conclusions when the purposefulness of God was only partially revealed. How silly I should be to walk through a theater and, from a few minutes' experience of the first act, make a deduction about the plot of the whole play or the character of the author. Yet, this is what we do about God.[1]

While I was serving as a chaplain in the United States Air Force, my family and I spent one of our overseas tours in Istanbul, Turkey. In the bazaars and shops we visited, we saw many beautiful and colorful Turkish rugs.

Today, most of the rugs are made on modern looms with modern equipment. But we were told that years ago large frames were set up and heavy thread, which makes up the base for the rug, was stretched between them. On the back side small boys were stationed at various levels with bundles of different colored yarn.

The skilled artist, working on the finished side of the rug, calls out his instructions to the boys. Each boy, with his own particular colors, weaves his threads into the pattern at the command of the artist.

When the artist calls for red, the boy with the red yarn weaves his thread into the pattern. When the need is for blue or black or green, the artist calls for those colors, and the boys weave them into the design. As each boy continues to add his color at the direction of the artist, the rug is completed in all of its beauty.

Each rug is different. No two patterns are alike. Each one presents a beauty and design all its own. All have their share of the bright colors as well as the darker ones.

The boys who work on the back side do not choose the colors because they cannot see the pattern. They follow the directions of the master weaver who sees the upper side. The boys who weave the drab colors may not prefer the shades, but they are needed just as much as the brighter ones. It takes all of the colors to make the pattern. Some are needed to highlight, and some to bring contrast to the others.

I suspect that this old poem attributed to Grant Colfax Tullar, with its various versions, is based on the ancient eastern rug-making art.

> My life is but a weaving
>   between my Lord and me;
> I cannot choose the colors
>   He worketh steadily.

Oftimes He weaveth sorrow
    And I in foolish pride
Forget He seeth the upper,
    and I the underside.

Not till the loom is silent
    and the shuttles cease to fly,
Shall God unroll the canvas
    and explain the reason why.

The dark threads are as needful
    in the Weaver's skillful hand
As the threads of gold and silver
    in the pattern He has planned.

Both C. S. Lewis and Leslie Weatherhead, in their books on suffering (*The Problem of Pain* and *Why Do Men Suffer?*), draw a parallel between God's concern for man and man's concern for his "best friend," the dog.

Though the comparison breaks down in a number of ways, the similarity is worth considering. Perhaps the following summary, based in part on the two books, will illustrate the idea of "Please Be Patient, God Is Not Finished with Me Yet."

Strangely enough, the Canary Islands were not named for those lovely yellow songbirds we call canaries. Rather, the name *Canary* was given to the islands because of the many ferocious dogs found there when the islands were first discovered in 40 BC. The early explorers referred to the islands as "Canaria" from the Latin name for dog, *canis*. The dogs that roamed the island were wild scavengers. They were savage beasts, devouring everything they found, sometimes even each other.

Were these animals happy in their snarling, biting, snapping state? One cannot reply with certainty. But most people would agree that today's well-trained, housebroken, disciplined, and obedient dog is a much better dog than the wild variety found on the islands. In our way of seeing things the wild dogs are far from being as well off as their domesticated cousins. The dogs did not reach their potential in the wild state. They were far from being what a dog could be in the hands of a patient and loving master.

But the question is, How does the dog get from one state of

development to the other? He cannot be expected to grow into a better dog just by following his natural inclinations. The change in the dog requires years of careful, selective breeding and training by some person. Without a trainer's help the dog would never be invited to share the warmth of this person's hearth or heart.

A trainer takes infinite pains to train his dog. Sometimes the dog is slapped with a newspaper in order to be housebroken. This will not hurt him, but it may frighten him. He will bathe the dog when he doesn't want to be bathed. The trainer may have to scold the dog to keep him from digging up the backyard.

Jerking on the leash during training in order to make the pet obey may cause discomfort. The master may have to cut down on the dog's feeding because he is getting too fat. Yet the dog would rather eat, since it is no fun going hungry whether you are a dog or a human being. All these things, and much more, go into the making of a well-disciplined, happy dog.

Why do all of this for a dog? Usually it is because the master loves it and wants to elevate the dog to a position of fellowship with himself. People usually don't have this kind of concern for an earthworm or a rattlesnake. Then why with a dog? It is because of the dog's capacity in the hands of a loving master. And the trainer will work with it in order for the dog to reach its highest potential.

Now, the similarity between an owner and his dog is far less than the similarity between God and human beings. And here it breaks down. The dog can never be like people, it is not in its nature. However, our Lord has made it possible for human beings to become like him ("As many as received him, to them gave he power to become the sons of God, even to them that believe on his name," John 1:12).

A person can grow toward the likeness of his Master, but it requires more than just following his natural leanings. It will require dying to self and what some may term suffering. And if Christ, the Son of God, was willing to suffer death on a cross because he knew the value of human beings, then we should be willing to continue that development toward the likeness of our Master.

Like the dog, we may become tired of all this concern and "bother" from God. We might wish that God had planned for us a far less glorious destiny, one more easily reached and with less discomfort involved. We might prefer to be left alone to follow our more natural leanings, to remain like we are. We might even wish God loved us only enough to leave us alone. But to ask God to leave us alone would be asking God to love us less, not more.

To the puppy just beginning its rigorous training routine, some of the things happening to him may leave the impression that his master is not a good person. In light of some of the things she has to undergo, it would not be unusual for the animal to ask, "If my master is a good master, why does he allow good dogs to suffer?"

I say it would not be unusual to hear this question. It is an understatement, for one hears it asked almost everyday. "If God is a good God, why does he allow good people to suffer?"

7

Lemons or Lemonade?

Cass Daley, a famous Hollywood comedienne, whose shouted songs and acrobatic contortions were a feature of Paramount musicals in the forties, attributed her success to the following philosophy of life: "When nature handed me a lemon, I made lemonade out of it." And nature did hand her a lemon—she was neither beautiful nor glamorous—but she made the best of a bad situation. She used her handicap to her advantage.

Someone has said it another way: "When fate tosses you a dagger, the important thing is how you catch it—whether by the handle or by the blade." The way we accept difficulties and disappointments in life is the important thing. Our attitude determines whether we will overcome our problem or be overcomed by it.

There was once a musician who suffered from very poor eyesight. His vision was so bad that it was almost impossible for him to read the musical scores. Because of his desire to excel, he worked long hours memorizing his parts. In fact, in order to become more sure of himself, he would even memorize the parts of the other musicians.

One day, just before a concert, the conductor became ill. There was no replacement. Because of his knowledge of the music, the half-blind musician was asked to fill in. The concert was a great success, so successful in fact, that this substitute director was asked to become the regular conductor.

Thus, one of the world's greatest symphony orchestra conductors, Arturo Toscanini, got his opportunity for greatness because he was not willing to let his poor eyesight defeat him. He overcame his suffering and rose to fame in spite of it.

The world is filled with many similar success stories. Books by the thousands have been written about men and women who overcame such handicaps or hardships. In most cases they succeeded, not despite their problem but because of it. It was the handicap that motivated them. It was their hardship that drove them on. It was their suffering that propelled them to heights they never would have attained otherwise.

When he was born, George W. Campbell was blind.

"Bilateral congenital cataracts," the doctor called it. . . .

And then, when George was six years old, something happened which he wasn't able to understand. One afternoon he was playing with another youngster. The other boy, forgetting that George was blind, tossed a ball to him. "Look out! It'll hit you!"

The ball did hit George—and nothing in his life was quite the same after that. Goerge was not hurt, but he was greatly puzzled. Later he asked his mother: "How could Bill know what's going to happen to me before I know it?"

His mother sighed, for now the moment she dreaded had arrived. Now it was necessary for her to tell her son for the first time: "You are blind." And here is how she did it:

"Sit down, George," she said softly as she reached over and took one of his hands. "I may not be able to describe it to you, and you may not be able to understand, but let me try to explain it this way." And sympathetically she took one of his little hands in hers and started counting the fingers.

"One—two—three—four—five. These fingers are similar to what is known as five senses." She touched each finger between her thumb and index finger in sequence as she continued the explanation. . . .

"George, you are different from other boys," she explained, "because you have the use of only four senses, like four fingers: one, hearing—two, touch—three, smell—and four, taste. But you don't have the use of your sense of sight. Now I want to show you something. Stand up," she said gently.

George stood up. His mother picked up his ball. "Now, hold out your hand as if you were going to catch this," she said.

George held out his hands, and in a moment he felt the hard ball hit his fingers. He closed them tightly around it and caught it.

"Fine, fine," said his mother. "I never want you to forget what you have just done. You can catch a ball with four fingers instead of five, George. You can also *catch* and *hold* a full and happy life with four senses instead of five—if you get in there and keep trying."

. . . George never forgot the symbol of "four fingers instead of five." It meant to him the symbol of hope. And whenever he became discouraged because of his handicap, he used the symbol as a self-motivator. It became a form of self-suggestion to him. For he would repeat "four fingers instead of five" frequently. At times of need it would flash from his subconscious to his conscious mind.

And he found that his mother was right. He was able to catch a full life, and hold it with the use of the four senses which he did have.[1]

However, the story of George Campbell's blindness doesn't end here. When he was in high school, an operation was developed for congenital cataracts, but it was new and untried. Relying on his philosophy of "four fingers instead of five," George Campbell was determined that he was going to see. And for that chance he was willing to face experimental surgery. After four painful operations over a period of six months, he received that "extra finger"—his fifth sense was restored; he could see.

Without an optimistic attitude toward their limitations, neither Toscanini nor Campbell would have overcome. They found victory not by sheer determination alone, but because they had an attitude that gave them determination.

"It is what you do with what you have—or don't have—that counts," goes the old cliché. But your attitude determines what you do with it. Attitudes makes the big difference.

One day an unknown short-story writer was accused of embezzling funds. The charges were denied. Nevertheless, he was sent to prison for three years. While there he determined to make "the best of a bad situation." All of his extra time was spent in writing. He developed and improved his style to the point that when he was released he became one of America's most famous short-story writers. His name? William Sydney Porter. But you will probably remember him better as O. Henry.

The next time you're feeling sorry for yourself because of some obstacle in life or because you believe a handicap is holding you back, I hope you will recall the story of Peter Gray.

Pick up any encyclopedia of baseball and you will find his name listed there among the baseball greats. Peter Gray, whose real name was Peter Wyshner, was born March 6, 1917, in Nanticoke, Pennsylvania. Nanticoke was the kind of town where smoke and coal dust painted the landscape and houses a dark, monotonous gray: A community where housewives fought an ever-losing battle against the soot and dust that settled on everything.

When Peter was very young, he had dreams of someday becoming a famous baseball player, but the rude reality of poverty indicated that his future would more likely be in line with that of his father and brothers, working in the mines.

One day Peter was in an automobile accident. He was very seriously hurt. The doctor said he would live but he would never be able to play baseball *or* work in the mines.

But Peter was not going to be defeated that easily. He might never work in the coal mines, but playing baseball was a different story. As he watched the other boys playing baseball outside his window, Peter became more determined than ever. Finally one day he persuaded them to let him play. It was only sand-lot ball, but Peter gave it everything he had. His playing won him a place on the local hometown club, the "Nanticoke Pit" team. With this encouragement he played even harder. Perhaps there might be a place for him in baseball after all.

Peter wrote a letter to Mel Ott in Miami. Mel wrote back with a casual invitation to drop by and see him someday. Peter took it for a specific invitation and headed for Florida. But after one look at Peter, Mel told him to go home and forget about baseball.

Peter would not be deterred. He went down to Philadelphia to see Connie Mack. Again the answer was the same as he received in Florida. They wouldn't even give Peter a try out.

Then one day things began to change. A baseball scout from the "Three Rivers Club" in Quebec saw Peter play. Impressed by his drive and determination, the scout recommended Peter. The manager sent for him; but again it was the same old hurtful rejection. No try out, but Peter was invited to watch a game from the bench, and that became the break he needed, for one of those seemingly insignificant things happened. A player failed to show up and Peter was asked to replace him in the line up. It was only a practice game, but that was enough. Peter played like his future depended upon this one game, and perhaps it did.

The bases were loaded when Peter came to bat. The pitcher threw and Peter's bat met the ball with a resounding crack that all but knocked the cover off. "Half way across Canada," someone said about the hit.

From now on it would be easier for Peter Gray to prove himself, and he would slug, and slam, and slide his way right up to the top: Finally to end up in the uniform of the St. Louis Browns.

It's all there in the records: The home runs, the stolen bases, his batting average, even the fact that he batted and threw left-handed. Nothing unusual about that; there are many left-handed ball players. But Peter Wyshner, who played under the name of Peter Gray, because of the auto accident as a young boy, played all of his games with a strong left arm and an empty sleeve where his right arm should have been.

Baseball has known many other players who have played with a handicap. Bert Shepard, who lost his right leg in the army, pitched for the Washington Senators in 1945, the same year that Peter Gray played for the Browns. Hugh Daly won seventy-two games in his career, and like Peter Gray he had only one arm. He pitched a no-hit, no-run victory and struck out nineteen players in one game. This is still an all-time record.

Harry Jasper was hit by a batted ball and lost an eye. Yet, this didn't stop him from playing several successful seasons of major league ball. Bill Irwin, who pitched for the old Cincinnati club, had but one eye. Tom Sunkel's left eye was blinded by a cataract, yet he played big league ball.

Mordecai Brown, a famous pitcher for the Chicago Cubs, had crippled fingers on his pitching hand, but like Clem Labin (mentioned elsewhere in this chapter) this proved to be an asset. It enabled him to grip the ball in such a way that he could throw a more effective curve.

Both outfielder Hal Peck and pitcher Charley Ruffing had several toes missing, but this did not hinder their playing.

All of these players either used their handicaps as a help instead of a hindrance, or overcame them by sheer determination.

> One ship drives east and another drives west
> With the selfsame winds that blow.
> 'Tis the set of the sails
> And not the gales
> Which tells us the way to go.[3]

When you are handed a lemon, make lemonade. It's what you make of your handicap, or problem, that matters. Whether your suffering in life grinds you down, or polishes you up, depends upon what you are made of.

The best solution to misfortune is to use it. Change it from a crushing blow of defeat to an upward jolt of victory. Transfer it from a negative drag holding you back to a positive power catapulting you forward. Use it as a stepping-stone instead of a stumbling block.

The cry of man's anguish went up to God,
    "Lord, take away pain!
The shadow that darkens the world Thou hast made;
    The close coiling chain
That strangles the heart: the burden that weighs
    On the wings that would soar—
Lord, take away pain from the world Thou has made
    That it love Thee the more!"

Then answered the Lord to the cry of the world,
    "Shall I take away pain,
And with it the power of the soul to endure,
    Made strong by the strain?
Shall I take away pity that knits heart to heart,
    And sacrifice high?
Will ye lose all your heroes that lift from the fire
    White brows to the sky?
Shall I take away love that redeems with a price,
    And smiles with its loss?
Can ye spare from your lives that would cling unto mine
    The Christ on his cross?"

—AUTHOR UNKNOWN

Jesus didn't just bear a cross; he used it. He used it to die on, to save a world lost in sin. He said, "I lay down my life, that I might take it again. No man taketh it from me, but I lay it down of myself. I have power to lay it down, and I have power to take it again" (John 10:17-18). Jesus was not a victim of the cross; he was a victor over the cross.

There are times when we feel we are victims of circumstances, that life has cheated us. We feel we have "missed out," been given "the short end of the stick." When this happens, often it is because we are guilty of comparing our lives with others. We are not thinking about what God has given us, but rather about what he has not given us—as compared to others, as we see them.

If we must make comparisons with others, then let's compare ourselves with those who have faced obstacles and overcome them. Both Mozart and Schubert composed many of their most beautiful pieces of music while deeply in debt and depressed because of poor health.

Beethoven, as many remember, was deaf when he composed his greatest music.

Goethe finished *Faust* during the final months of his life, knowing that death was near and his time was short.

Milton wrote *Paradise Lost* after he had gone blind.

Cervantes, who wrote *Don Quixote*, did not do his greatest works until after he lost an arm in the battle of Lepanto.

Although in failing health, Mark Twain, author of *Tom Sawyer* and *Huckleberry Finn*, never let his suffering keep him from writing some of his most famous humorous literature.

Handel wrote his famous oratorio the *Messiah* while facing loss of popularity and plagued by bankruptcy and failing health.

Francis Parkman, the American historian, suffered so severely from pain during the greater part of his life that he could work for only a few minutes at a time. And his eyesight was so poor, he wrote his manuscripts by scrawling a few giant words on each page.

Louis Pasteur, the scientist who gave us pasteurization, did many of his experiments while semiparalyzed and under the constant threat of apoplexy.

While ill and unable to move from her bed, Florence Nightingale reorganized the hospitals of England.

During the time Charles Dickens was writing his most brilliant novels, he was being pressured constantly by editors and troubled by financial and marital problems.

It took Michelangelo six years to complete *The Last Judgment*; during that time he suffered almost continually from internal physical disorders and pain. His pseudobiography, written by Irving Stone, is well entitled *The Agony and the Ecstasy.*

But one does not have to go back into history to find heroes who have overcome their handicap and become successful. As examples, in the music field there are Ronnie Milsap, Ray Charles, Stevie

Wonder, Johnnie Ray, Jose Feliciano, and many others. All of these entertainers are blind with the exception of Johnnie Ray, who is hard of hearing and wears a hearing aid.

It is a common mistake to think of a handicap as an enemy of success. A disability can be a teacher—a harsh one, but a good one.

"Afflictions are but one shadow of God's wings," wrote George MacDonald.

Recently, I found in my files a newspaper article about George Waldhart. During World War II he lost four inches off his leg when a German shell exploded near him. He spent twenty-seven months in the hospital before he was released.

Doctors told him he would never be able to walk without a steel support. But within two years he threw the brace away.

Fifteen years later he lost his right arm and part of his shoulder in a farming accident: while working alone on a hay baler in a remote area his glove became caught in the machine, pulling his arm and shoulder between two metal rollers.

"For ten or fifteen seconds," he said, "I just gave up on life."

Then he swears he heard a voice telling him: "Fight, fight this thing!" So he raised up, pulled himself clear, and left his arm and one shoulder in the machine. He used his left arm to pack his jacket into the area where his shoulder had been and walked a mile to a nearby farm. There the farmer gave him a ride into town to a hospital.

"I never lost consciousness," he said, "but when I walked into the hospital emergency room the nurse took one look at me and fainted."

What is George Waldhart doing now? At the date of the article he was working on the police force for the city of Gallatin, Tennessee. He was fifty-four years old and able to handle a variety of assignments. Primarily his job was writing traffic tickets. He said he wrote from forty-five to fifty citations a day.

What does he think about his loss? His philosophy is, "I'm not giving up." However, he will admit he had had to overcome one real obstacle. The thing that almost got him? Learning to write with his left hand.

The difficulties of life either make us bitter or better, depending on the way we face the problem.

When Fanny Crosby was six weeks old and suffering from an

illness, someone put the wrong medicine drops in her eyes, and she was blinded. Later in life she could have easily become bitter. But her mother taught her that blessings, both to the sufferer and to others, can come out of suffering. She kept reminding her daughter of many famous poets who were also blind.

Fanny Crosby eventually became a great Christian poet herself. In her ninety-four years of life she was a blessing to many people. Many of her great gospel songs are in church hymnals today, where her work has continued to bless millions.

Another great Christian, George Washington Carver, faced with the poverty and frustration of slavery, overcame his difficulties and rose to become a scientist and a "saint." His philosophy was: "Don't cry for what you haven't got; take what you have, and make something out of it." He did this with the lowly peanut and the common sweet potato and developed hundreds of valuable products from them.

Napoleon Hill tells us that there is a law of life that says: "Every adversity, every unpleasant experience, every failure, carries with it the seed of an equivalent or greater benefit." Or as the old proverb goes, "Every cloud has a silver lining."

Take the story of Clem Labine for instance. Clem Labine is known throughout the baseball world as a pitcher who can throw one of the best curves in the game: a jug-handled curve. When Clem was a young boy, he broke the index finger on his right hand. The finger was not set correctly. It healed, but there was a permanent crook between the first and second joints. Clem was already deeply interested in baseball, and he became discouraged. It seemed to him that this was the end of his dream of a baseball career. . . .

"Don't be so sure," his coach told him. "Sometimes the things that seem like disasters turn out to be blessings in disguise. It all depends on how you regard the troubles that come your way. It is said that *every adversity has the seed of a great benefit.*"

Clem took the advice to heart and kept playing. Soon he discovered that he had a natural pitching arm, and as he practiced he found that the crooked finger could be put to good use. The bend gave the ball a twist and a spin that no other pitcher on his team possessed. Clem was encouraged. Year after year he worked to develop this spin until he became one of the really fine pitchers of our day.

How did he accomplish this? Through natural skill, to be sure; through hard work, of course; but even more important—through a change in mental attitude. Clem Labine had learned to look at the good in his unfortunate situation.[3]

Do you remember Joseph, Jacob's favorite son (Gen. 37 ff.)? His own brothers betrayed him and sold him as a slave. Down in Egypt he was arrested on false charges and thrown into prison. He could have become bitter and allowed the gnawing pains of resentment to consume him. But he took his wrongs and turned them into rights. With an unwavering faith in God he accepted a bad situation and let God change it into a good situation.

Elevated to a position next to Pharaoh, Joseph became a blessing to the whole country of Egypt. His own family, including his brothers who sold him into slavery, were saved from starvation. Thus, he saved the people that were to eventually become the nation of Israel.

Joseph was handed a lemon, but he used it to make lemonade. These words, spoken to his brothers, reflected this attitude: "But as for you, ye thought evil against me; but God meant it unto good, to bring to pass, as it is this day, to save much people alive" (Gen. 50:20).

When you are discouraged and feel things are not going your way, open the Bible and turn to this story of Joseph. It begins in the thirty-seventh chapter of Genesis. Joseph is one of the great personalities of the Old Testament. He is an overcomer. Many of the great saints of the Bible are people who suffered and won. They let their suffering make them, not break them.

Are you facing hardships? Don't despair; it may be the making of you. Someday you may look back and thank God for allowing you to carry the burden you are bearing.

I have a friend who was with me in the Air Force Chaplaincy School at Lackland Air Force Base in Texas. He had been a missionary in Korea. When the North Koreans overran the country, he was taken prisoner along with some other American missionaries and a number of Koreans. I credit this story to him.

Soon after their capture, the prisoners were driven unmercifully on a forced march to the North. Because of the lack of food and rest they became exhausted and discouraged. They trekked through snow, day after day, and the bitter cold bit deep into their bones.

One old man found it difficult to keep up and kept dropping behind the marching column. Finally, when he could go no longer, he lay down beside the road in a snowbank.

As the prisoners moved on down the road they knew they were

leaving him to die. They could not carry him, and he would not walk. Soon he would be frozen there beside the road. The guards did not seem to care. The group saw no way to encourage him or to force him to keep going.

Suddenly one of the mothers broke away from the rank of slow-moving prisoners. She ran back to the old man sitting in the snow, too tired and too cold to move. She tried to pull him up; she shouted words of encouragement. It was no use. Then she took her own small baby from off her back, laid him down in the lap of the old man, and hurried back to join the group.

The guards and their prisoners stopped to watch. Soon the old man struggled to his feet, and with the small bundle in his arms, he wearily trudged on to catch up with the group.

That evening when they reached camp, the old man with trembling arms, reached out, and embraced the mother. With muffled sobs he said, "Thank you . . . thank you for putting that burden in my hands."

8

The Pruning of the Vine

I know of no other plant that runs into unproductive wood as quickly as the grapevine—(that must be where the expression "deadwood" came from). When the branches of the grape are not pruned, they stop producing fruit and begin producing only wood. Probably no plant needs to be pruned as frequently or as much as the grapevine.

In the area of California where I live there are thousands of acres of grapes. In the fall they are harvested and made into California's famous wines. After the harvest, when the leaves have fallen, one can look out across the field and see only a wilderness of tangled branches. Then sometime before spring, workers move along the rows cutting back the vines, almost to the ground it seems. The tangled mass of branches are hauled off and burned. The stubby trunks with only a few buds are all that remain. It seems the pruners must surely have killed the vines. But when spring comes, the buds burst out into a vigorous growth of new leaves and fruit. It is the beginning of another good vintage year.

Jesus said, "I am the true vine, and my Father is the husbandman. . . . Every branch that beareth fruit, he purgeth it, that it may bring forth more fruit" (John 15:1-2). He could not have used a better example than the grapevine to illustrate our need for spiritual growth through "pruning" or chastisement.

Chastisement is an interesting word. It comes from the Latin word *castus* and means "to purify" or "to make chaste." So when God allows us to be chastised through suffering, we are not being punished. Rather, he wants us to be changed for the better.

"My son," writes the author of Hebrews, "despise not thou the chastening of the Lord, nor faint when thou art rebuked of him: For whom the Lord loveth he chasteneth" (Heb. 12:5-11). This passage mentions two things about chastisement: we are not to despise or ignore it—take a stoic attitude. Neither are we to faint or become discouraged because of it.

Chastisement is the mark of sonship. Just as an earthly father chastens his children, so our Heavenly Father chastens us. Chastening, or disciplining, is never done out of unkindness but always because God cares. It is a sign of love.

Discipline has a slightly different meaning than the word *chastisement*—though God often uses both. *Discipline* basically means "to learn." (The word *disciple* comes from the same root word.) Discipline is a teaching exercise; chastisement is a purifying process.

A group of small boys were playing baseball. It was late, long past the hour when one young fellow should be home. But because the game was so interesting, he refused to answer the call to come in.

Finally, someone from one of the houses went hurrying across the playing field. He rushed over to one of the boys, turned him over his knee, and spanked him. "Now, get your glove and come in this instant!" he ordered.

As the boy ran across the field one of his small friends asked, "Who was that?"

"Who do you think it was, stupid? That was my dad! Who else would do that to me?"

It would be well for parents to remember that when they chastise or discipline their children they are showing responsibility. Many child psychologists agree that children need a "firm hand" if they are to feel secure and loved.

Remember, it is the roughness of the grindstone that sharpens the ax. It is the storm that hardens the fibers of the oak. It is the workday and not the holiday that builds muscles.

The baby chick hatching from the egg is not helped when someone else peels away the eggshell for him. He must be allowed to develop the strength that comes from pecking his way out of his own prison cell. Any attempt to make it easier for him only hurts the chick.

When I was a small boy, I found a moth cocoon out in a field. I took it home to keep through the winter, hoping to see a colorful creature emerge in the spring. Sometimes I wondered if a moth were really

something better through one's pain. (This point was discussed more fully in chapter 1.)

Augustine once wrote: "The cost of the kingdom requires no other price than yourself. Give yourself for it, and you shall have it." The principle is clear: to gain that which is best costs us the pain of losing that which is good.

And, at the time, we may be aware only of the pain, like the oyster and the grain of sand. But like the pearl, God is working out something of beauty and value in our lives.

I read a story of a boy and his boat the other day. Again, this simple story illustrates the idea of this chapter.

A small boy had built a toy boat. Proud of his work, he went off to a lake in the park to sail it. Soon it was beyond his reach and finally it drifted to the center of the lake and stopped. Seeing no way to retrieve it, he began to cry. An older boy who was watching came to his rescue and began throwing rocks in the direction of the little boat. The little fellow was sure now that the boat was lost. It would be sunk at the hand of the other boy. He began to cry even harder.

Then, through his tears he saw that the rocks were not falling on the boat, but beyond it. Each wave from the splashing rocks moved the little boat closer to the shore. That which he thought was to be the loss of his boat was its means of rescue.

How many times do we judge the rocks which fall into the quiet waters of our life to be only for our ruin? We see them falling as though without rhyme or reason. But wait! Like the little boy and his boat, we will see that they are falling with purpose and plan.

Many beautiful psalms were written during a time of suffering. As the psalmist faced these trials in his life he also found a closeness to the Good Shepherd.

David, who wrote the twenty-third Psalm, reminds us that there are not only green pastures and still waters to enjoy, but there is the rod and the staff. Both the rod and the staff were well known in the pastoral life of the shepherd.

The rod was a short stick that hung at the shepherd's side. It was used primarily to protect the sheep against the danger of wild animals. However, it was not unusual for the shepherd to use it upon the sheep, in a more gentle way. He would use it to herd them into the fold at night or to drive them back onto the path when they had strayed.

Of course, the staff was the familiar shepherd's crook. It was used to direct the sheep by reaching ahead and tapping them a soft blow on either side of the shoulder. The loop or crook was also used to retrieve a stray lamb out of a brier patch, or off a ledge. The crook was hooked around the animal's neck, and he was simply lifted up. Painful? Somewhat. But the temporary suffering rescued him from a greater harm.

When we suffer, we are usually not as submissive as sheep. Many times we cry out to God, "Why am I being punished?" But our suffering is not always equated with punishment. (Punishment is a penalty for an offense, and not necessarily corrective.) We may be suffering, not because we have been bad but for just the opposite reason. God is allowing something to happen in our lives to make us even better. Remember, God's own Son, Jesus Christ, suffered as no other man.

Tribulation is another word used to describe suffering and sorrow. It can be redemptive in nature. It comes from the word *tribulum*. This was the instrument used to thresh wheat. It divides the grain from the chaff, the good from the bad. Tribulation can be a separating, a cleaning, or refining process.

God spoke to Israel concerning their suffering through Isaiah, the prophet. He said, "Behold, I have refined thee, but not as silver; I have chosen thee in the furnace of affliction" (or tribulation) (Isa. 48:10).

David, in Psalm 66:10, wrote "For thou, O God, hast proved us: thou has tried us, as silver is tried."

How is silver tried?

In the days when these passages were written, the refiner would continually remove the impurities from the surface of the liquid metal. As the dross was removed, the glistening beauty of the silver began to shine through until finally the molten metal became like a mirror. When the refiner was able to see his own image reflected in the pure silver, he knew the refining was complete.

This parallels what happens in our lives when God allows us to be chastened through afflictions. Satisfaction must fill God's heart when he begins to see his own image reflected in us. As fire is to the silver, so chastisement is to our life.

The apostle Peter wrote, "Beloved, think it not strange concerning the fiery trial which is to try you, as though some strange thing happened unto you" (1 Pet. 4:12). Suffering can be the "fiery trials" through which we are purified.

This is a compliment to God's children since it compares them to precious metal. In the fire they will not be destroyed, but only refined. We are not like "wood, hay, and stubble" (1 Cor. 3:12), but like "gold and silver." Fire destroys flammable things but refines and purifies enduring metals.

It is said that in the days of sailing vessels, builders carefully chose the right wood for their ships. For the all important keel, the finest seasoned timber was used. It was cut from a tree that grew in a high place, exposed to the weather: a tree that had been twisted by hurricanes, and on whose branches the heavy snows of winter had lain. The shipbuilder wanted a tree that had been bent many times and straightened up again without breaking. Perhaps if we under- stood our tribulations and trials as the seasoning of "God's timber," we could bear them better.

As I look around at the great saints in my own church, they are the ones who have been bent by suffering and straightened up again. They are the ones who show the greatest love toward God and the most concern for their neighbors.

There is an old French proverb that says, "Suffering will pass away, but not to suffer will never pass away." Suffering is painful, but only temporary, and what we learn cannot be experienced any other way; neither can it be taken away.

> I walked a mile with Pleasure,
> She chattered all the way,
> But left me none the wiser
> For all she had to say.
>
> I walked a mile with Sorrow,
> And ne'er a word said she;
> But, oh, the things I learned from her
> When Sorrow walked with me![3]

When we study the Book of Job we realize that Job's loyalty to God could not be proved until Job faced trouble. Until tested, his faith would remain only a theory.

God knew that Job would stand the test, but Satan did not know this, and Job was probably not sure. But Job faced it and came out victorious. As painful as testing is, we will never know how we will respond until we have faced the experience. There is no other way to prove it.

When my family and I lived in New England, often we drove up into Maine at the time of apple harvest. Maine apples are regarded as among the best in the world—at least those who live there tell you so. They also tell you that sometimes apple trees suddenly stop bearing fruit and produce only wood and leaves. When this happens the owner will often take a drastic step to change the nature of the tree. He will wound the tree by cutting deep gashes along the trunk. Almost every time—and no one knows why—the tree will turn its bearing strength back to producing fruit. Like the tree, sometimes we are allowed to be "wounded" in order that we might bear "fruit" instead of "wood and leaves."

Somehow this reminds me of the man who prayed for God to give him patience. But all God gave him was more problems to solve, and more hardships to endure. Yet, how else could God have given him more patience except by giving him those things that develop patience?

The apostle Paul wrote, "We glory in tribulations also: knowing that tribulation worketh patience" (Rom. 5:3). And James wrote, "My brethren, count it all joy when ye fall into divers temptations; Knowing this, that the trying of your faith worketh patience" (Jas. 1:2-3).

Someone has said concerning answered prayer: "I prayed for strength that I might achieve; I was made weak that I might obey. I prayed for wealth that I might do greater things; I was given infirmity that I might do better things. I prayed for riches that I might be happy; I was given poverty that I might be wise. I prayed for power that I might have the praise of men; I was given infirmity that I might feel the need of God. I prayed for all things that I might enjoy life; I was given life that I might enjoy all things."

In his sermon "Going Up to Jerusalem," Phillips Brooks said: "O, do not pray for easy lives. Pray to be stronger men. Do not pray for tasks equal to your powers. Pray for powers equal to your tasks."

> Our Father, when we long for life
> without trials and work without diffi-
> culties, remind us that oaks grow strong
> in contrary winds, and diamonds are made
> under pressure.

> With stout hearts may we see in every
> calamity an opportunity and not give
> way to pessimism that sees in every
> opportunity a calamity.[4]

9

"If,"
the Saddest of Words!

"If" is a mighty big word,
If an elephant had wings
He'd be a mighty big bird!

This little nonsensical poem was popular when I was a boy. When someone used the word *if* as a prefix to a wishful thought or an excuse, this would be our retort.

I learned the weight of that little word early in life. If! Yet, many times since, I have found myself using it in wishing for an impossible return to the past. "Oh, if I had only done it differently . . . If I had waited . . . If I had only known." In looking back at some major decision, I longed to go back and choose another way.

We make ourselves miserable as we think of what might have been. Remorse is painful: perhaps the most agonizing of all emotional sufferings. Missed opportunities and regret, creating an almost unbearable anguish of soul and spirit.

Nor ear can hear nor tongue can tell
The torture of that inward hell![1]

"If I had only made another choice. If I had left earlier—or later. If I had only gone the other way. If I had only known. If I had taken more time—or less time." How often we look back at the past and torture ourselves with such words or thoughts. But the past is past; it is gone forever. Nothing can bring it back.

The Moving Finger writes; and, having writ,
Moves on: nor all your Piety nor Wit
Shall lure it back to cancel half a Line,
Nor all your Tears wash out a Word of it.[2]

Since we cannot alter the past, reviewing an unpleasant memory is not only futile but once again, through association, we experience the same painful emotions. We become like the little boy whose uncle promised him five dollars on the condition that the little fellow not think of "elephant" for the entire day. Did he get the money? Of course not. The five dollars and the elephant were too closely related. Association was certain. Remember one, and he remembered the other.

Not only are we hurting ourselves when we dwell on the past, but we tend to paint "that which might have been" in brilliant hues. We include no drab colors. The scenery along the road not taken is always brighter, and we never see the detours.

I have traveled the "if road" of the past many times. For a number of years I was a pilot with the United States Air Force. When God called me to be a minister, I gave up my flying career. I resigned, reluctantly, but with the bitter joy of self-sacrifice. And for some time after, when a jet went screaming overhead, I would look up and remember my loss. I would recall the carefree life, the shorter hours, the excellent pay. . . . I was guilty of putting my "hand to the plough, and looking back" (Luke 9:62). Remembering a good yesterday I often forgot the goodness of today.

However, I forced myself to remember I had made a choice between two careers, and I could not dictate the future of either. As I thought of beautiful days and smooth flying, I needed to realize there would have been stormy days and rough flying as well. To be honest, should I not, in my imagination, picture my plane one day slamming into the side of some desolate mountain peak? The headlines: "Plane Crashes, Passenger and Crew Perish!" After all, this, too, is a part of flying.

Had I not done what I felt was God's will for my life, perhaps this could have been my fate. I would have become a graphic illustration for a fellow pastor's sermon. "I remember when God called him into the ministry, but he refused. If he had done what God wanted, and not what he wanted, he would not have been flying that plane." Foolish conjecture? Yes, perhaps! But, isn't one assumption just as valid as the other?

Maud Muller by John Greenleaf Whittier is a beautiful example of the bittersweetness of memory wedded to imagination. The poem contains these famous lines, "For of all sad words of tongue or pen, the saddest are these; it might have been!" Here is the main part of the poem.

Maud Muller on a summer's day
Raked the meadow sweet with hay.

Beneath her torn hat glowed the wealth
Of simple beauty and rustic health.

Singing, she wrought, and her merry glee
The mock-bird echoed from his tree.

But when she glanced to the far-off town,
White from its hill-slope looking down,

The sweet song died, and a vague unrest
And a nameless longing filled her breast,—

A wish that she hardly dared to own,
For something better than she had known.

The Judge rode slowly down the lane,
Smoothing his horse's chestnut mane.

He drew his bridle in the shade
Of the apple-trees, to greet the maid,

And asked a draught from the spring that flowed
Through the meadow across the road.

She stooped where the cold spring bubbled up,
And filled for him her small tin cup,

And blushed as she gave it, looking down
On her feet so bare, and her tattered gown.

"Thanks!" said the Judge; "a sweeter draught
From a fairer hand was never quaffed."

He spoke of the grass and flowers and trees,
Of the singing birds and the humming bees;

Then talked of the haying, and wondered whether
The cloud in the west would bring foul weather.

And Maud forgot her brier-torn gown,
And her graceful ankles bare and brown;

And listened, while a pleased surprise
Looked from her long-lashed hazel eyes.

At last, like one who for delay
Seeks a vain excuse, he rode away.

Maud Muller looked and sighed: "Ah, me!"
That I the Judge's bride might be!

"He would dress me up in silks so fine,
And praise and toast me at his wine.

"My father should wear a broadcloth coat;
My brother should sail a painted boat.

"I'd dress my mother so grand and gay,
And the baby should have a new toy each day.

"And I'd feed the hungry and clothe the poor,
And all should bless me who left our door."

The Judge looked back as he climbed the hill,
And saw Maud Muller standing still.

"A form more fair, a face more sweet,
Ne're hath it been my lot to meet.

. . . .

He wedded a wife of richest dower,
Who lived for fashion, as he for power.

Yet oft, in his marble hearth's bright glow,
He watched a picture come and go:

And sweet Maud Muller's hazel eyes
Looked out in their innocent surprise.

. . . .

She wedded a man unlearned and poor,
And many children played round her door.

But care and sorrow, and childbirth pain,
Left their traces on heart and brain.

And oft, when the summer sun shone hot
On the new-mown hay in the meadow lot,

And she heard the little spring brook fall
Over the roadside, through the wall,

In the shade of the apple tree again
She saw a rider draw his rein;

And, gazing down with timid grace,
She felt his pleased eyes read her face.

. . . .

Then she took up her burden of life again,
Saying only, "It might have been."

Alas for maiden, alas for Judge,
For rich repiner and household drudge!

God pity them both! and pity us all,
Who vainly the dreams of youth recall.

For of all sad words of tongue or pen,
The saddest are these: "It might have been!"

Ah, well! for us all some sweet hope lies

> Deeply buried from human eyes;
> And, in the hereafter, angels may
> Roll the stone from its grave away![3]

Does not this poem, set in the frame of our own experience, bring nostalgic memories to each of us? We look longingly back down the road we have come and wonder "what might have been." But we cannot build upon such fragile foundations as our imagination.

There is a sequel to the poem "Maud Muller" written as a parody by Bret Harte. It is a reminder that if we were able to choose again, we might not be too happy with the alternate choice. If we could see far enough down that other road, we might again choose the one we traveled.

The poem is entitled "Mrs. Judge Jenkins: Sequel to Maud Muller."

> Maud Muller all that summer day
> Raked the meadow sweet with hay;
> Yet, looking down the distant lane,
> She hoped the Judge would come again.
> But when he came, with smile and bow,
> Maud only blushed, and stammered, "Ha-ow?"
> And spoke of her "pa," and wondered whether
> He'd give consent they should wed together.
> Old Muller burst in tears, and then
> Begged that the Judge would lend him "ten;"
> For trade was dull, and wages low,
> And the "craps," this year, were somewhat slow.
> And ere the languid summer died,
> Sweet Maud became the Judge's bride.
> But on the day that they were mated,
> Maud's brother Bob was intoxicated;
> And Maud's relations, twelve in all,
> Were very drunk at the Judge's hall.
> And when the summer came again,
> The young bride bore him babies twain.
> And the Judge was blest, but thought it strange
> That bearing children made such a change:
> For Maud grew broad and red and stout;
> And the waist that his arm once clasped about
> Was more than he now could span. And he

Sighed as he pondered, ruefully,
How that which in Maud was native grace
In Mrs. Jenkins was out of place;
And thought of the twins, and wished that they
Looked less like the man who raked the hay
On Muller's farm, and dreamed with pain
Of the day he wandered down the lane.
And, looking down that dreary track,
He half regretted that he came back.
For, had he waited, he might have wed
Some maiden fair and thoroughbred.
For there be women fair as she,
Whose verbs and nouns do more agree.
Alas for maiden! Alas for judge!
And the sentimental,—that's one-half "fudge;"
For Maud soon thought the Judge a bore,
With all his learning and all his lore.
And the Judge would have bartered Maud's fair face
For more refinement and social grace.
If, of all words of tongue and pen,
The saddest are, "It might have been,"
More sad are these we daily see:
"It is, but hadn't ought to be."[4]

Harte was no sentimentalist. The philosophy of his poem may shock our sensitivity, but it has a ring of candid reality about it. Honestly, isn't this the way many of our romantic dreams of "what might have been" would probably have ended?

One thing that causes remorse is seeing the past in light of all the accumulated knowledge of the present. We blame ourselves for not having prophetic vision and forget that we acted on the best information at hand. The memory of the details that influenced our decision become dull with time. Faced with the same set of circumstances, we would probably act again in the same way.

During World War II, my crew and I were forced to parachute from a disabled plane over the Himalayan "Hump." (It was out of this experience that I came to trust Christ as my personal Savior, but that is another story.) All four of the crew got out of the plane safely. Our parachutes opened, and we landed in the highland jungles of Burma near the border of China.

With the exception of the radio operator, the crew soon made contact with one another by wading down the middle of a small stream. The three of us set up camp at a fork in the creek and waited, hoping that the radio operator would soon come down one of the stream's branches. Also, the area where the stream forked was the best open place where we could be spotted from the air. We waited for the air drops and began to make plans for our trek back to civilization.

We had abandoned our plane early in the morning; and within thirty minutes after we dropped into the jungle, rescue planes were crisscrossing the area. But they were concentrating their efforts on the other side of a ridge. Each time they came over our area they were turning and could not see us.

By early afternoon clouds began to blanket the area, so no more rescue attempts could be made that day. Since there was nothing to do but wait, we made the best of the situation. There were fish to be caught in the stream, and we enjoyed a long swim. We lighted a fire to dry our clothes and to cook our food. At evening we made a tent from one of the parachute canopies, and settled down for the night. The only thing needed to make our "outing" a little more complete was the rest of the crew, the radio operator.

During the night, a steady rain began to fall. By nine o'clock the next morning the stream was a swollen torrent. Because of the weather, our hope for any help from the air was gone. There was no assurance that the rain would let up, either that day or that week or that month. It was the beginning of the monsoon season, and no planes would be out searching for us.

We knew what we would have to do. Even though it meant leaving the radio operator, we would have to float out of the jungle. (We had already concluded that the radio operator had landed on the other side of the ridge and was not in the same valley with us.) To cut our way over to him through the thick tangle of vines would have been almost impossible and too time-consuming. The only way one could move through the dense jungle was down a stream, as we had done the day before.

We began to build a raft from the giant bamboo that grew along the stream; within a few hours it was finished. We launched our frail craft and were soon on our way, bobbing along like a cork, dipping and whirling down the swollen stream. The camp area was soon far behind us.

Our decision to float out of the jungle by way of the stream had been a practical one. By late afternoon we floated into a jungle survival training camp that had been established by the United States Army—to train men in exactly what we had just experienced. Soldiers soon drove us to a nearby airstrip, and we were flown back to our home base at Myitkyina, Burma. After arriving back at the base camp, we spent the next day writing a detailed report of our experience, including our feelings and thoughts.

Two weeks later the radio operator, exhausted and bleeding from lacerations and leeches, staggered out to the famous Burma road and was rescued. We were thankful he had been found alive, but regretted we had not been able to bring him out with us. Had we done so, we could have saved him from the hardships he suffered.

A number of years later, I began to develop a feeling of guilt for having left one of my crew members in the jungle. I asked myself, *Why didn't we search for the radio operator and bring him out with us?* It seemed so reasonable later. But did it seem reasonable at the time? I searched through the files and reread the report written while the events were still fresh in our minds: Leaving him there seemed, at the time, to be a logical decision. We didn't know how long it would take us to be rescued by air. The decision to float down the stream was a frightening choice—the trip was more like shooting rapids than floating. Once we pushed out into the stream we could not return: We were at the mercy of the current. Overhanging vines would sweep us off our raft into torrential water. Our raft plowed into submerged rocks and flipped over time and time again. We lost our few supplies; at times we almost drowned. We became wet and cold and hungry. Our greatest concern was that the stream might suddenly disappear underground, sending us whirling into some water-choked cavern; or we would tumble end over end down some towering waterfall.

If we were able to get out, we had decided we could personally direct rescue efforts from the air when the weather cleared. After all, we knew the radio operator's position, and we felt we knew better than anyone else how to find him, and get him out.

In reviewing the written report I found, rather than feeling sympathetic for the radio operator, we were almost envious of him. Before the clouds had covered the hillside, we were sure several planes had dropped supplies into his area. (We were correct. The rescue squadron confirmed the drops. However, because of the dense jungle, the radio operator had been unable to retrieve any of the supplies.)

We discovered from the report that our first thoughts of slashing through the jungle to find the radio operator were based more on a desire to share in his supplies rather than to rescue him. We were disappointed that all of the drops had been concentrated on his area and not in our direction.

As I write this, a feeling of regret resurfaces out of my subconscious to bother me. Without having an account of the crew's thoughts and feelings at the time to refer to, as aircraft commander I might still be overwhelmed by a sense of guilt and remorse for having left the radio operator.

It's easy to be a Monday-morning quarterback, even in the area of being critical of our own past decisions. It is easy to decide today what should have been done yesterday.

What should we do with memories? If they are pleasant, we need to cherish them; however, if they are unpleasant, and there is nothing we can do to change them, we should try to forget them. Psychologists tell us that we can develop a strong tendency toward forgetfulness. (Remember that unpleasant phone call you dreaded making and somehow forgot? Or that appointment you didn't look forward to and missed.) The fact that the things we often forget are unpleasant is more than a coincidence. In the same way, we can purposefully forget unpleasant memories or poor decisions.

When an unpleasant memory of a past mistake forces its way into your consciousness, look at it for a moment. If you did your best, admit you made the best decision under the circumstances with the knowledge you had at the time, then forget it. If, however, you did less than your best and there is guilt, confess it. Seek forgiveness (both from the one you hurt, if possible, and from God). Once this is done, don't spend time questioning your forgiveness.

The reason we are plagued by feelings of remorse is because we bring up the past and nurse our grief. Dwelling on the past will not help relieve the anguish of regret or heal the wound of a past hurt. Continuously looking back and reliving the past is somewhat like a small boy who keeps unwrapping the bandage on his sore toe, opening and exposing the wound again, causing it to heal slower.

I clipped the following from Ann Landers' syndicated column for March 8, 1972. I think it illustrates the point in a practical way.

Dear Ann Landers: I'm 21 and feel 91. The problem is I can't get over a lost love. I don't want to be melodramatic about it but I honestly believe a broken heart can be physical as well as emotional. I actually feel a pain in my heart. No need to go into the details, but I can never get him back.

I have passed up chances to date because I'm so blue I'd be lousy company. After work I come home and play our favorite records. I read and re-read his notes, letters, and poetry. I look at the photographs of us together. And I cry myself to sleep. How can a girl go on when her whole life has come apart at the seams? I need help. — Mood Indigo.

Dear M: Get rid of all those relics reminiscent of the past. If you don't want to destroy them, put them out of your reach. Force yourself to accept dates. Push all thoughts of your lost love out of your mind. Easy? Of course not, but it's the only way you'll come out of your half-dead state and start to live again. Get going and good luck.[5]

It can be done. I have a sister-in-law whose son was a prisoner in Cuba. His plane had been forced down, and he was imprisoned on false charges. Having put his safety into the hands of God, she trained herself not to be anxious or to worry about him. She was not being hardhearted. She remembered him in her daily prayers, but she was determined not to wring her hands in frustration, knowing this would only add to her suffering. She knew that to dwell on "what might have been" or to imagine "what was going to be" would not help. And since the mind responds only to what it experiences, and because the mind cannot tell the difference between the real and the imaginary, she would not allow her imagination to control her life.[6]

The idea of dismissing the past with all of its painful regrets is not new. The apostle Paul blended forgetting and faith into a very practical mixture. Brethren, I count not myself to have apprehended ["arrived"]: but this one thing I do, forgetting those things which are behind, and reaching forth unto those things which are before, I press toward the mark for the prize of the high calling of God in Christ Jesus (Phil. 3:13-14).

So . . .

> Take the proverb to thine heart,
>   Take, and hold it fast—
> "The mill cannot grind
>   With the water that is past."
>   —SARAH DOUDNEY

10

Praise the Lord, Anyhow

For a number of years, a walnut plaque inscribed with the words "Praise the Lord, Anyhow" sat on my desk. It was given to me by my son when he was in college. When he handed me the plaque, he told me a story to go along with it:

"Dad," he said, "sometimes when I am driving along the highway and my old car breaks down [he had a 1959 Chevrolet at the time—it would be a classic today], I get awfully discouraged, and I wonder, 'Now, why did this happen to me?' Then I look in the rearview mirror, back down the road, and I think of all the miles that old car has brought me. And I say, 'Praise the Lord, anyhow.'"

I have thought of these words many times. This is the way we ought to accept suffering when it comes our way. We should have the attitude of "Praise the Lord, anyhow!" We may not understand it; but, despite the circumstances, we ought to remain faithful and not blame God. "Praise the Lord, anyhow," regardless of the situation. Despite the fact the Bible does not tell us the full meaning behind suffering (although it gives some broad principles), it does show us that this should be our attitude.

In the Old Testament the prophet Habakkuk looked around and saw all the suffering come upon his people and asked that familiar and agonizing question, "Why?"

The question was all the more significant because his country was being destroyed by a people more wicked than themselves. How could God stand by and watch the righteous get swallowed up by the wicked? His country Judah may not have been a perfect nation, true, but it certainly was not as evil as the Chaldeans, who were about to overrun them. Where was justice? Though Habakkuk did not find the answer to the "Why" of suffering, he nevertheless found the answer of "How" to accept it.

Although the fig tree shall not blossom, neither shall fruit be in the vines; the labour of the olive shall fail, and the fields shall yield no meat; the flock shall be cut off from the fold, and there shall be no herd in the stalls: Yet I will rejoice in the Lord, I will joy in the God of my salvation (3:17-18).

Consider another familiar Old Testament example: the story of three Hebrew children who were cast into the fiery furnace because they would not worship a golden idol. Thanks to a song the names of the young men are well known, but the words that express their faith in the goodness of God are not nearly as familiar:

Shadrach, Meshach, and Abed-nego, answered and said to the king, O Nebuchadnezzar, we are not careful to answer thee in this matter. If it be so, our God whom we serve is able to deliver us from the burning fiery furnace, and he will deliver us out of thine hand, O king. But if not, be it known unto thee, O king, that we will not serve thy gods, nor worship the golden image which thou hast set up (Dan. 3:16-18).

Here is a faith that says, "We believe that our God will save us, but whether he saves us or not, he is still our God, and we will be true to him." This is the same kind of faith expressed by Job. In the face of all his undeserved suffering, he still cried out: "Though he slay me, yet will I trust in him" (13:15).

Of course, the greatest example of one's willingness to accept and go through suffering is found in the agonizing prayer of Jesus in the garden of Gethsemane. It was on the eve of his crucifixion that he prayed, "Father, if thou be willing, remove this cup from me: nevertheless not my will, but thine, be done" (Luke 22:42). The answer to suffering is found in a continual faith in the goodness of God and not in the answer to the question "Why?"

Because of Jesus' continued faithfulness—even the death of the cross—he has blessed countless millions. In writing to the Christians at Philipi, the apostle Paul said, "Let this mind be in you, which was also in Christ Jesus: . . . And being found in fashion as a man, he humbled himself, and became obedient unto death, even the death of the cross" (Phil. 2:5,8).

One rendering of the life of Jesus that has impressed me is entitled "One Solitary Life."

Here is a man who was born in an obscure village, the child of a peasant woman. He grew up in another obscure village. He worked in a carpenter shop until He was thirty, and then for three years He was an itinerant preacher.

He never wrote a book. He never held an office. He never owned a home. He never had a family. He never went to college. He never put His foot inside a big city. He never traveled two hundred miles from the place where He was born.

He never did one of the things that usually accompany greatness. He had no credentials but Himself. He had nothing to do with this world except the naked power of His divine manhood.

While still a young man, the tide of popular opinion turned against Him. He was turned over to His enemies. He went through the mockery of a trial. He was nailed to a cross between two thieves. His executioners gambled for the only piece of property He had on earth while He was dying—and that was His coat. When He was dead He was taken down and laid in a borrowed grave through the pity of a friend.

Nineteen wide centuries have come and gone and today He is the centerpiece of the human race and the leader of the column of progress.

I am far within the mark when I say that all the armies that ever marched, and all the navies that were ever built, and all the parliaments that ever sat, and all the kings that ever reigned, put together, have not affected the life of man upon this earth as powerfully as has that One Solitary Life.

What was the secret of the victorious life of Jesus? He lived a life totally committed to the goodness of God. He was faithful in all situations and did not doubt, despite suffering and sorrow.

Ella Wheeler Wilcox's poem "Faith" illustrates the belief in the total goodness of God in a very poignant way:

I will not doubt, though all my ships at sea
     Come drifting home with broken masts and sails;
     I shall believe the Hand which never fails,
From seeming evil worketh good to me;
     And though I weep because those sails are battered,

Still will I cry, while my best hopes lie shattered,
   "I will trust in Thee."

I will not doubt, though all my prayers return
   Unanswered from the still, white realm above;
   I shall believe it is an all-wise Love
Which has refused those things for which I yearn;
   And though, at times, I cannot keep from grieving,
   Yet the pure ardor of my fixed believing
     Undimmed shall burn.

I will not doubt, though sorrows fall like rain,
   And troubles swarm like bees about a hive;
   I shall believe the heights for which I strive,
Are only reached by anguish and by pain;
   And, though I groan and tremble with my crosses,
   I yet shall see, through my severest losses,
     The greater gain.

I will not doubt; well anchored in the faith,
   Like some stanch ship, my soul braves every gale,
   So strong its courage that it will not fail
To breast the mighty, unknown sea of death.
   Oh, may I cry when body parts with spirit,
   "I do not doubt," so listening worlds may hear it
     With my last breath.

While serving as an air force chaplain some years ago, I received a heartbreaking phone call from a young airman and his wife. Their baby daughter had suddenly died of the mysterious "crib death."[1] I was at a loss as I tried to comfort these grieving parents. What could one say? But with tears on his face, the young airman said to me, "Chaplain, we have agreed that we can't change what has happened. But we can choose the way we are going to accept this. Turning from our belief in God's goodness will not remove our sadness; instead, it will just deny us the strength to overcome it. All we have left is God. But when you have him, that is all you need."

I have just finished reading Dr. Arthur John Gossip's sermon, "But When Life Tumbles In, What Then?" It was the first sermon he preached after the sudden and unexpected death of his wife. I was struck by the similarity between his advice, fresh from his own experience with death, and the conclusion of this young couple.

In his message he said: "I do not understand this life of ours. But still less can I comprehend how people in trouble and loss and bereavement can fling away peevishly from the Christian faith. In God's name, fling to what? Have we not lost enough without losing that too? . . . You people in the sunshine may believe the faith, but we in the shadows must believe it. We have nothing else."[2]

Today medical science may be close to finding the cause and cure for crib death (SIDS). As I read of the progress being made, my mind goes back to that lonely couple who stood in the corner of a Cape Cod cemetery and wept at a small open grave. Today I wonder if they know that their loss, coupled with thousands of others, has finally made us aware of the need for research in this area. Perhaps the reason for these deaths will soon be found. Then thousands of babies will be saved and thousands of parents will be spared this grief. In a very, very small way that young couple's suffering may prevent the suffering of others. But most important of all, they were not to be defeated by something they did not understand. They trusted God, anyhow.

The philosophy of old "Uncle John" is worth considering. It expresses a right attitude about life. John was often plagued by illness, injury, and financial loss. He seemed to have more than his share of the problems of the world. But nothing was able to defeat him. He met every morning with, "Good morning, Lord, thank you for another day." He always greeted his friends with a broad and happy smile.

When asked one day: "How can you always be so cheerful, John?"

His brief answer was, "I have learned to cooperate with the inevitable."

He was saying, "Praise the Lord, anyhow!"

A father loses all that he has in a business venture. His family suffers privation. The mother must go to work; the daughter drops out of college and gets a job; the other children wear the same old clothes and shoes to school. Do you know that the greatest thrill that can come to that father is to have his family's love, and see them stand by him? This says to the father, "We love you for what you are, despite the way things have gone for us." In the same way, as God's children, we must continue to trust our Heavenly Father, and not turn from him in the face of disappointments and suffering.

If serving God automatically guaranteed only good things—health, money, success, life free from problems, no suffering—then logically everyone would turn to God. But to think this way assumes that God deals only in physical commodities, things that can be touched and seen. This is not God's modus operandi.

Jesus said, "Therefore I say unto you, Take no thought for your life, what ye shall eat, or what ye shall drink; nor yet for your body, what ye shall put on. Is not the life more than meat, and the body than raiment?" (Matt. 6:25).

Charles Haddon Spurgeon, the great English preacher, in his famous sermon "Songs in the Night" said:

"Any fool can sing in the day. When the cup is full, man draws inspiration from it; when wealth rolls in abundance round about him, any man can sing to the praise of a God who gives a plenteous harvest, or sends home a loaded argosy. It is easy enough for an Aeolian harp to whisper music when the winds blow; the difficulty is for music to come when no wind bloweth. It is easy to sing when you can read the notes by daylight; but the skillful singer is he who can sing when there is not a ray of light to read by—who sings from his heart, and not from a book that he can see."

A short time after Dr. Daniel A. Poling lost his son Clark in World War II (one of the four chaplains mentioned in an earlier chapter, who gave up their life belts when their ship was torpedoed), he was visited by a mother whose own son was in the same war and was in combat at the time.

In the course of the conversation she said, "I know that God is good, and he loves my son. So I believe he shall return safely." Dr. Poling smiled and said kindly, "Whether your son returns or not, the love of God and his goodness is not at stake. We must continue to trust him."

"Praise the Lord, anyhow!"

11

It's Your Face, Face It!¹

"I'm so ugly! Look at me! I wish I were dead." These are the disparaging thoughts of many young people today. They suffer from a negative self-image. In an age when the entertainment and commercial world places such a high premium on personal attractiveness, failure to measure up can cause a real concern.

However, this low esteem of oneself is not restricted just to young people. For unless something is done early in life to improve one's attitude, negative self-criticism will continue on into adult life. One usually doesn't grow out of it.

For such people, self-criticism becomes a habit. When watching a movie, or television, or thumbing through a magazine, they are making comparisons. When walking across the campus or seeing a school play, they are constantly comparing themselves to others.

As they become more occupied with their own appearance they become less friendly toward others, and often appear to be sophisticated or independent. This causes rejection and contributes even more toward their low self-esteem. The cycle continues—spinning ever inward toward a center of self-rejection.

Some young people have become so depressed because of their low self-esteem that they have actually committed suicide. Many crimes and other forms of antisocial behavior can be traced back to resentment of others brought on by self-rejection. It is not just a coincidence that many violent acts against society are committed by those who have a physical appearance considered to be less desirable by social standards. But whether it results in outward hostile behavior or inward retreat, the blight on the personality cannot be ignored.

Bill Gothard, director of the Institute of Basic Youth Conflicts, feels this problem is so serious that he gives a full session to it in his training program. From his work among young people he has concluded: "A person's attitude toward himself has a profound influence on his attitude toward God, his family and his friends, his future, and many other significant areas of life."[2]

Probably the most critical area to be affected is the person's attitude toward God. She often fails to realize that her self-criticism is also a criticism of God, her creator—for to reject the design is to reject the designer. In her rejection, she is actually saying to God: "You did a poor job on me, and I resent it."

Resenting the way God has ordered things, a person feels cheated by the Creator. Feeling let down by God, one becomes bitter and distrustful. If God can't be trusted in this area, how can he be trusted in other areas?

This becomes rebellion—typical of the attitude expressed in Isaiah 45:9. "Woe unto him that striveth with his Maker! . . . Shall the clay say to him that fashioneth it, What makest thou? or thy work, he hath no hands [handle]?" Or as expressed in Romans 9:20-21, "Nay but, O man, who art thou that repliest against God? Shall the thing formed say to him that formed it, Why hast thou made me thus? Hath not the potter power over the clay, of the same lump to make one vessel unto honour, and another unto dishonour?"

In the Book of Job,[3] the justice of God is brought into question because of Job's suffering. But God reminds Job that in the case of "Job *vs.* God," Job's criticism is based upon limited knowledge. God reminds Job that there are many things he does not know, and in chapters 38 and 39 God lists them one after the other. In light of this rebuke, Job admitted that there were gaps in his knowledge and he ceased to argue his case.

In light of our own limited knowledge, we have no other choice but, like Job, to clamp our hand over our mouth. We are in no position to argue because we don't have all the evidence.

Young people are seldom aware that self-rejection is rebellion against God, nor do they realize how serious it is. In addition, when one desires the physical features of another, he breaks the Tenth Commandment; he is guilty of coveting. This is a word seldom heard today, but we see its results all about us. It is a desire to want that which belongs to another, a greed for that which is not our own.

Although coveting usually refers to material things, the desire to be like someone else—real or imaginary—is coveting. Coveting makes us unhappy, and sometimes we grow to hate the one whose features we cannot have.

When one cannot accept oneself, it is difficult to accept others. Friends become mere yardsticks by which to measure oneself as "more than," "less than," or "equal to." A person may feel comfortable only with those who do not exceed his standards. He develops a "birds of a feather . . . misery loves company" complex. Many school fights and other aggressive conduct can be traced to this attitude. In answer to the question, "Why did you hit him?" The reply is often, "I just didn't like his looks."

People's ideas of what looks good changes with the times. Therefore, it is better to realize that you are a unique person than to be depressed over the fact that you don't fit the going idea of what looks good to society at the moment. Not everyone can be a muscle-bound-movie-star type hero. Nor can many look like the models in advertisements and television.

How do we make the most of what we are? How do we overcome that feeling of worthlessness? How do we change a negative self-image into a positive one?

First, face reality. This can be terribly painful, but the pain is temporary. You will gain a certain satisfaction when you are honest with yourself. Besides, when you really face your problem, you may find it is not nearly as bad as you had feared. You will have peace when you surrender and accept the way God made you. For peace usually comes when fighting ceases. It's your face (or whatever your problem), so face it. Face the futility of trying to change things that cannot be changed.

This does not mean that there is no need for self-improvement. Face up to your problem squarely, and you may find that there are things you *can* do to improve yourself. Let this little prayer be your prayer:

God, grant me the grace to accept the things I cannot change, and the courage to change the things I can change, and the wisdom to know one from the other.[4]

In the Sermon on the Mount, Jesus asked facetiously, "Which of you by taking thought can add one cubit unto his stature?" (Matt. 6:27). What was he saying? It is foolish to waste energy on things that cannot be changed. As an example he said, "No matter how much you 'worry and fret' you cannot change your height." There are things that cannot be changed. It is much better to accept them and move on. Of course, Jesus was not referring just to height, but anything that cannot be changed. (However, if height is your problem, and you want to be taller, here are some figures I saw the other day: If God didn't make you six foot, don't worry. Remember, there is only a nine percent difference between being five foot six inches, and six feet.)

David Young, a nuclear physicist at Stanford University, in Palo Alto, relates the following story which helped him to understand and accept the limitations God has given all of us:

When I was a small boy I lived on a farm here in California. I loved the outdoors, and I spent every minute that I could exploring the wonders of nature in the hills that surrounded our valley.

One afternoon I was walking along the top of a high ridge and I spotted a hawk in a tall tree that leaned away out to overlook our fertile acres. I saw a nest in that tree, and I felt sure that there must be some eggs in that nest. I wanted those eggs so badly, but I knew it was impossible to reach that nest without breaking the tree limb and falling down the mountainside.

So I closed my eyes and prayed. I prayed for God to let me fly up to that nest just like the hawk so I could get those eggs. And as I prayed, I thought that I ought to show God I had some faith, too, so I flapped my arms up and down as fast as I could just like wings. I was so sure that God would hear my prayer and answer it, but, of course, nothing ever happened.

And then the hawk flew into the air so gracefully from the nest. I was so envious. But as it flew away, a feeling of understanding came over me, young though I was, that God could not interrupt or change the orderliness of His creation so that little boys might fly.

From then on I think I knew deep down inside of me that to be happy, one had to follow his inner guidance so that he might do that which God had given him the talent to do. And that he should also accept the limitations that had been placed upon him as exactly that—limitations—and nothing more. Only then could a person realize his true potential, do great things, and fulfill his own individual destiny.[5]

However, even with your limitations you are someone special. No one else is exactly like you. There has never been, and there never will be anyone else like you.

Just as fingerprints differ, so people differ. God makes no carbon copies. Each of us is a new individual, a separate creation. As no two snowflakes are alike, so no two people are ever identical either. No two leopard skins are identical in their markings. Every leaf on every oak tree differs. When God made you, he used a pattern that was to be used only once. You are unique.

You were born a champion! Have you ever thought about the battles you won before you were born? "Stop and think about yourself," says Amram Scheinfeld, an expert on genetics.

"In all the history of the world there was never anyone else exactly like you, and in all the infinity of time to come there will never be another." You are a very special person. And many struggles took place that had to be successfully concluded in order to produce you. Just think: tens of millions of sperm cells participated in a great battle, yet only one of them won—the one that made you! It was a great race to reach a single object: a precious egg containing a tiny nucleus. This goal for which the sperms were competing was smaller in size than the point of a needle. And each sperm was so small that it would have to be magnified thousands of times before it could be seen by the human eye. Yet it is on this microscopic level that your life's most decisive battle was fought.[6]

Today there is great emphasis on the hobby of bottle collection. In fact, it has become more than a hobby; it is now a business with many thousands of dollars invested in various collections.

On weekends, collectors by the thousands drive to the hills and deserts. There they search out old garbage dumps, rubbish piles, and abandoned homes with the hope of finding old and rare bottles. Considered worthless at one time, they were thrown away; now, they are in great demand; some are almost priceless. What changed their value?

As with most items, such as coins and stamps, it is not the age but the rarity that determines their worth. How many others are there like it?

For a number of years my wife and daughters bought toilet articles in beautifully designed bottles. They were usually thrown away when empty (though not without a regret, for how could something so beautiful be so worthless?). Now many of these same bottles have become valuable collectors' items. What has made the difference? Again, the value is based on their scarcity and design. The manufacturer produced only a few of each pattern; then the mold was broken. Because only a limited number was made, those that were saved became valuable.

Remember, like the bottles, when God made you, he broke the mold. But unlike the manufacturer, he uses only one design for each person. That is how rare an individual you are.

The Bible teaches the importance of these individual differences. In one of the early churches, some were stressing one person's ability over another. Writing to them, the apostle Paul compared their various differences to the numerous parts of the body that are all needed. He wrote:

For the body is not one member, but many. If the foot shall say, Because I am not the hand, I am not of the body; is it therefore not of the body? . . . If the whole body were an eye, where were the hearing? If the whole were hearing, where the smelling? . . . And the eye cannot say unto the hand, I have no need of thee: nor again the head to the feet, I have no need of you (1 Cor. 12:14-21).

Of course, Paul was referring to the spiritual body of Christ; but it does not violate the spirit of the illustration to say that in his great scheme of things God desires us all. Not only does he desire us, but he uses our individual differences that make us so unique.

Before World War II, I worked for a large aircraft plant in San Diego, building flying boats for the US Navy. The company used a team of dwarfs to work inside some of the cramped wing sections. Those men were the only ones small enough to do the work. Their size was their biggest asset; normal men could not squeeze into the areas.

We have all read of the heroic acts of small men who have risked their lives by descending into wells or mine shafts to rescue children that have been trapped. Because of their size, they have been able to perform deeds of bravery which no one else could do.

When we are discouraged and tempted to think of ourselves as of little value, we should remember these words of Jesus: "Did ye never read in the scriptures, The stone which the builders rejected, the same is become the head of the corner: this is the Lord's doing, and it is marvellous in our eyes?" (Matt. 21:42). Jesus was applying this to his own rejection and crucifixion. But he knew there would be victory in the resurrection, and millions would receive him as Lord.

His illustration was based on an interesting story concerning a small building block which lay unused during the construction of the great Jewish Temple. Lying around in the dust, it seemed to have little value. However, when the Temple was almost completed, one space remained. It was discovered that this small, rejected stone fit perfectly into the final gap. That which had been unimportant, suddenly became the most important stone in the Temple, joining all the other stones together.

There is a place in life's building for each of us. We are needed. No one else can fill that space. Each of us was made to fit into a particular spot. But we will never find our niche in life until we enter into a personal relationship with God, "the Master Builder."

How do we begin making our relationship personal? Remember what was said earlier? Face up to reality! Second, we need to go one step further. We need to thank our "Designer."

"Thank him?" Yes, thank him despite your limitations and problems. "Thank him? For what? I may be able to accept things as they are, but to thank God? Never!"

Until you can thank him you are still rebelling against your "Designer." "Well, I can thank him that I am no worse than I am." No, not that way either. You must thank him that you are you and not someone else. Ask him to forgive you for rejecting his design. True, you would have preferred to be different—and you would have been different had you anything to say about the matter. But our physical appearance is in God's hands, and we developed according to his plans—not ours. "It is he that hath made us, and not we ourselves" (Ps. 100:3).

Abraham Lincoln was not physically attractive. Yet Mr. Lincoln never let this become a problem to him. In fact, at times he seemed to delight in his homely appearance, and emphasized it. One old story indicated that Mr. Lincoln not only accepted his appearance, but was also thankful.

An artist, commissioned to paint a portrait of the great man, tried to be kind to Mr. Lincoln and omitted some of the blemishes on his face.

When Mr. Lincoln saw the work, he studied it for a few moments and objected, "Paint me just as I am, warts and all!"

So, it's your face, face it.

12

The Meshing of Gears

One of the promises of the Bible is that God can use suffering to bring about good. Like the meshing, or engaging of gears in an automobile, suffering can bring things together and produce blessings. Though suffering is not good, good can come out of suffering.

When gears are properly brought together, energy can be transferred; and work can be done. In a similar way, suffering is able to mesh with other things and bring good into our lives.

Suffering is compensating; it makes amends. It is like an exchange, the swapping of one thing for another. Hurt is swapped for good.

Even Newton's law of motion seems to apply to suffering. Newton's third law simply stated is, "For every action there is an equal and opposite reaction." Applied to suffering, one can say that an equal, or greater, amount of good can come from our suffering.

For every negative there is a positive. A plus compliments a minus. For every up, there is a down. For every loss there is a gain. For bad there is good. And out of suffering there can come a greater blessing. There are good things that we cannot have or know except through the experience of suffering.

Here are two stories that illustrate this truth. Notice how the good and the bad are buffeted back and forth.

One classic example, written by Ivan P. Tewarson of India, was printed in the daily devotional magazine the *Upper Room* for October 20, 1960.

The story is told about an Indian king who lost one of his fingers while on a hunting trip. Told by his friend that God does everything for the good of mankind, the king became very angry and threw his friend into a dry well.

Soon after, some bandits caught the king and took him away to be sacrificed. But realizing that he was not an acceptable sacrifice, because of the missing finger, the bandits released him.

He quickly returned to the well and pulled out his friend, ashamed and repentant for having thrown him in. The friend said to the king, "It was good you threw me into the well; otherwise, I myself surely would have been captured by the bandits and sacrificed."

The other illustration concerns a shipwrecked survivor who landed on an uninhabited island with a few meager supplies he was able to salvage from the ship. There he built a small hut in which to store his few provisions and to protect him from the weather. Each day he searched the horizon for a passing ship.

One day after hunting for food on the opposite side of the island, he returned to find his hut in flames. All of his provisions, everything he had saved, was lost in the fire. Life had only been a bare existence before; now he saw no hope. He thought God had completely forsaken him, but he held onto his faith.

A bit later a ship came steaming across the horizon toward his island. "We saw your smoke signal and have come to your rescue," said the captain.

These anecdotes exemplify what the apostle Paul meant when he wrote: "We know that all things work together for good to them that love God, to them who are called according to his purpose" (Rom. 8:28). We know that he is talking about suffering because of what was written just before this famous passage. He is not saying that suffering is good. And, of course, he is not denying the reality of it. He knew better! He had seen Christians lose everything—often their lives. Instead, he is saying, "Hold on to your faith, for even suffering will work for your good. Things will one day fit together—mesh—to form a pattern for good."

However, Paul did not say suffering will work for good in everyone's life. He modifies his statement by outlining specific conditions. The principle applies only to those who love God and are part of the pattern in his great plan.

Have you heard someone say after some tragedy or loss, "Well, the Bible says all things work together for good"? We would all like to believe this. But this quotation, out of context, isn't even a good half-truth. Things *do not* work for good to those who rebel against God and do not love him.

Let me show you how suffering can result in good. Do you remember the story of the Turkish rug in chapter 6? Sometimes the boys working on the reverse side of the rug put in the wrong color of yarn. The mistake is not intentional, just carelessness.

Does the artist make the boys remove the thread? Usually not! Not if he is a great artist. For the greater the artist, the better he can weave the misplaced color into the pattern, and it will be more beautiful than planned. In fact, it is said that one of the tests of a genuine antique Turkish rug is that it will have some irregular colors woven into the pattern.

In the same way God says to us: "If you are mine and will trust me, I can take those handicaps, those disappointments, that hurt, that pain—all—and weave them into the pattern of your life. And, it will be more beautiful than if you had not suffered.

Suffering might be compared to two chemicals. Apart they may be poisonous. But, when brought together in the right way, something good is produced. The new compound will be greater than the sum of the two.

Sodium and chlorine are good examples. One is a dangerous mineral, the other a poisonous gas. Chemically combined they form common table salt. Alone, neither has a place in our home. But together, they produce a necessary seasoning and preservative for use in the kitchen.

It seems that God, that great bookkeeper, has a double-entry system for his children. On the debit side of the ledger he records our suffering, but on the credit side he records our blessings that come because of suffering. Of course this oversimplifies the matter, but suffering is not without purpose or reward. God knows how to weave it into the overall "big picture," for our good, if we remain faithful and continue to trust him.

God can bring blessings out of suffering, praise out of cursings, and good out of evil. He can take an evil person, who seems utterly useless and, through Jesus Christ, change that person into a saint. This is the message of the gospel. The world says, "You have made your bed, so you must lie in it." There is no forgiveness, no second chance. But Jesus said, "No, 'Take up thy bed, and walk' "—your sins are forgiven; you have a second chance. He is the Great Salvager.

Consider the death of Jesus. Who would have looked for any blessing to come out of that first Good Friday? (The very name itself, "Good Friday," has been given to the day because of this good-bad paradox.) It looked like it was all evil, all bad, all suffering, void of any good.

The disciples were almost convinced that he was who he claimed to be. He was not like other men. His teachings, his miracles, his healings—had they not all proved his authority? Surely he was the Messiah. Surely he was their great leader and conqueror.

But that afternoon his body slumping on the nails of the cross, looked like anything but a leader and a conqueror. Bruised, battered, and bleeding, he hung pale and limp in death on Golgotha's hill.

So he was as other men! Death had defeated him. He could not overcome this last great enemy of mankind. With his death went all of the disciples' hopes and plans. No wonder they fled in fear and scattered like leaves in a fall breeze. This was the end!

After thirty-three years this man from Galilee had found rest—but it was the rest of death and seeming defeat.

But on the third day something happened. The women came hurrying back from the tomb, claiming a most fantastic story. "The stone has been rolled away. The body is gone. The grave clothes not disturbed. He has risen from the dead!"

This is the greatest example of defeat and victory in the world, the changing of bad into good. At the resurrection God changed death into life, suffering into glory, and hate into love. And people have never tired of telling the story.

Because of Jesus's victory through the cross, people have been changed. Cowards have become heroes. Weak persons have become strong. Reeds shaking in the wind have become like pillars of steel. All because of Jesus. Could anyone question the great good that came out of the cross? God made the suffering of Jesus into the greatest of blessings.

Tonight I read the story of a man who, with his young wife and two sons, moved to another country. They left their home because of hard times, but in the new land they found hope for a better life.

Then tragedy struck! The husband died, and the wife was left alone with her two sons. They matured and married lovely wives. Life was full again. But tragedy struck once more. One son died . . . then another. Except for her daughters-in-law, the wife was left brokenhearted and alone.

Deciding to return to her old homeland, she began the journey with her two daughters-in-law. On the way one of them left her and went back to her own country.

The homecoming for Naomi and Ruth was not a happy one. The widow, though God fearing, was bitter and disappointed with life. When old friends saw her, they commented on her change. Her life had become so colored by suffering that she would not hide her sorrow; in her bitterness she even changed her name.

Could any good thing ever come out of this disappointment and tragic loss?

The two women struggled along; it was a hand-to-mouth existence. Then good fortune came to the young girl. She met a rich farmer in the community. They were married and in time a son was born.

After the birth of the son, the older woman's bitterness was changed to joy. She was so happy that the neighbors said she acted like the boy was her own. She knew in her heart that one day he would become a great man, that God had a great plan for his life.

And God did! He became the grandfather of a great king. Not only that, but he was to become the forefather of the supreme King, our Lord and Savior Jesus Christ.

You can read the story in the Bible; it is found in the Book of Ruth: the grandmother was Naomi; the young mother, of course, was Ruth; and the young son was Obed, the grandfather of King David, an ancestor of Jesus.

Did sorrow come to Ruth and Naomi in order that this great blessing might happen? Or did God bless them because of their suffering? Could the good have happened without the bad? One thing is certain, the blessings far outweighed the sorrow that the two women experienced. What a privilege to have one's name recorded in God's holy Word. And what an honor to have been an earthly ancestor of both the great King David and our Lord.

During the summer I often visited my son, Jon, and his family who lived at the Grand Canyon National Park in Arizona. He was the pastor of a church that has a unique ministry on the rim of the canyon.

Summer was a very busy season for him with four church services on Sunday, nightly concerts, and a large group of summer missionaries to house, feed, and care for. All of this and more is a part of the church's attempt to offer a spiritual "cup of cold water" to some of the two million people who visit the Grand Canyon between Memorial Day and Labor Day. (A literal cup of cold water is equally a part of the church's ministry as they provide water by the barrels-full to the thirsty tourists.)

I was always impressed by the large number of wholesome, clean-cut young men and women who came to the canyon to spend their summers with Jon, working as summer missionaries. One year as I was being introduced to the staff, I noticed one young girl in particular. She was very attractive, her face radiated happiness, and there was a sparkle in her eyes, enthusiasm in her voice, and sincerity in her smile; but she had only a "flipper" where her arm should have been (later, I was told she had an artificial leg as well). I soon learned that she was one of the thousands of "thalidomide babies" whose mothers took the tranquilizer drug during pregnancy, resulting in certain deformities, usually the limbs of the children. Many of the mothers felt justified in aborting their pregnancy because of the probability of the birth of a deformed child.

As I observed this young girl singing and performing during the concerts, it was apparent that she had not only overcome her physical handicap, but she had used it in a marvelous way in developing a dynamic personality. I thought, what a great loss if her parents had taken the "easy way out" and not allowed this lovely girl to be born. What a blessing this young girl must be to her parents despite the disappointments they faced and difficulties they had to cope with in the early years.

A similar illustration can be brought even closer to home. My daughter Kathleen, who is a professional model, is in frequent demand as a speaker at mother-and-daughter banquets. She often tells the story of another young girl and a mother's love, a mother who was willing to spend a great amount of time in bed in order not to terminate a pregnancy. Despite the lack of encouragement from her doctor, the mother hung on tenaciously to her one strand of hope, as she continued to reinforce her faith by prayer.

"Even if the child's life were saved, the baby might be a monstrosity," warned the doctor. "This was natures way of correcting an abnormal pregnancy."

But the mother would not give up. Finally the baby was born, and though there had been severe damage and scarring to the placenta, the baby was a healthy and normal child. Despite the hardship of many months in bed, and the doubts and questioning by the parents, any sacrifice they were called upon to make was minor compared to the life of this child.

My daughter usually concludes the story with these words: "That mother? That child? That was my mother; and I am that daughter. I'm that 'monstrosity' whose life my mother saved."

The stoning of Stephen, the first Christian martyr (Acts 6:7-8), was a great infraction of justice—"a terrible mistake." But it was probably because of Stephen's death that the apostle Paul became a Christian, thus giving us much of the New Testament.

As Paul stood and watched the stoning, he must have been deeply impressed by the courage of this young follower of Jesus. His suffering must have made a deep impression upon Paul, and, perhaps, led to his conversion to Christianity. It could probably be said, "Had Stephen not died physically, Paul might not have lived spiritually."

Sometimes it is hard for us to understand why God allows certain things to happen in our life. But even when tragedy strikes, God can use it like the meshing of gears.

There is a very interesting story of how we got our English Bible. It bears out this truth of the "meshing of gears."

While William Tyndale was secretly working on his English translation of the Old Testament from the Hebrew, he was betrayed into the hands of his enemies. King Henry VIII had him arrested and imprisoned. After two years the king ordered that Tyndale be executed. He was tied to the stake, strangled, and then burned. Grateful for the opportunity to suffer for his Lord, Tyndale's last words were, "Lord, open the eyes of the king of England."

Tyndale's death had a profound effect on the king. A year later the Bible was published throughout all of England, and the people, instead of being denied the Bible, were instructed to read it. The order was given by the same king, Henry VIII. So Tyndale's prayer was answered; his suffering was not in vain, and his death was not without meaning.

Billy Bray, who lived hundreds of years after Tyndale, was confident that God worked this principle in the lives of his children, even to the smallest of details. He believed that all things, good or bad, worked to the advantage of those who loved God. Here is a humorous account in his life that illustrates the meshing of gears.

The new chapel at Kerley Downs lacked a pulpit. Given six shillings, Billy was sent to the auction to buy a cupboard to serve as the preacher's stand. Unfamiliar with auction tactics, he bid the whole six shillings to open, and despite his pleading, saw another man walk off with the cupboard for seven.

Stunned, Billy trudged home. Passing a house, he saw the man from the auction trying to twist and maneuver the cupboard into his house. It wouldn't go. The frustrated buyer was ready to cut it into kindling wood when Billy rushed up and offered him six shillings if he would transport the cupboard to Billy's chapel. The man thankfully agreed, and Billy sighed, "Praise the Lord! He knew I had no way to get the cupboard to the chapel so he had you haul it for me. It's just like my Heavenly Father."[1]

No wonder Billy Bray was called, "God's glad man of Cornwall."

Charles Spurgeon was one of the great Christian preachers of the last century. As a young man he made an appointment to meet with a college professor to discuss a career of teaching in a college. They were to have met at a certain roadside inn. When Spurgeon arrived he was shown to a room to wait. Presently the professor came, and the same young lady showed him to another room. Each waited. Finally the professor left without meeting Mr. Spurgeon.

When the young woman realized her mistake, she apologized to Mr. Spurgeon and asked his forgiveness. But he interrupted: "My dear young lady," he said, "that is perfectly all right. God was in this, and God never makes a mistake."

As a result of the missed meeting, Mr. Spurgeon forgot the thought of a college career and went on to become one of the greatest preachers of his time.

Spurgeon often said afterward concerning the event, "Had I not missed that interview I might never have become the vessel that God meant me to be. But God was in it. Blind chance or accident has no place in the life of God's people."

One of the most beautiful stained-glass windows in the world may be seen in a church in Europe. When the artist had finished making all the other windows, he was left with thousands of worthless pieces of broken, colored glass. Rather than throw them away, he designed a window, and with these fragments made the most glorious and beautiful window of all.

In the same way God can take the worthless, broken pieces of our lives and build something glorious and beautiful.

When we are surrendered to God, he takes those things that break our hearts and fragment our lives, and brings wholeness out of them.

Someone has said concerning our suffering, "God can mend a broken heart if we will give him all of the pieces." But you have to love God and want to be in his plan. You can't keep back part of your life for yourself. You have to give him "all of the pieces."

Jesus said, "If any man will come after me, let him deny himself, and take up his cross, and follow me" (Matt. 16:24.) Denying ourselves involves giving up all claim to our life; and our cross, like Jesus' cross, will involve suffering. It is a mixed metaphor, but the old-time evangelist was right when he said, "Every cross you bear is molding you for a crown to wear."

A young couple faced the tragic death of their small daughter. After the funeral they returned to the loneliness of their empty home. Arm in arm they walked into the little girl's room. There on the wall hung a small plastic cross with a few words beneath it. They had scarcely noticed the words before, but in the light of their loss they were more meaningful than ever. At the bottom of the cross they read, "The cross glows in the dark." How true. Jesus is never more real than in the dark hour of our suffering.

A number of years ago, five missionaries were killed in South

America. It happened on January 8, 1956. The martyrs were Nate Saint, Jim Elliot, Roger Yonderian, Ed McCully, and Pete Fleming. All five were killed by the Auca Indians deep in the Ecuadoran jungle near the Curaray River. The story is well known in the annals of missionary work. Rachel Saint (sister of Nate Saint) and Betty Elliot (wife of Jim Elliot) have written a number of books about the five men; so I will not go into a lot of detail.

But, briefly, the story is this: For months careful preparation had been made to contact a savage tribe of Auca Indians living deep in the Amazon jungle.

After detailed planning and concentrated prayer, these five pioneer missionaries felt the time of contact had come. They flew into the area and landed their small plane on a sandbar along the river. There they waited for further contact from the tribe. Three days later the first contact that white man had ever made with the Aucas was recorded.

Pete Fleming wrote in his diary: "My heart jumped and thumped wildly as three Aucas, two women and a man, stepped out into the open on the opposite bank."

The men reported the meeting on the radio and said that they were on the verge of meeting ten or more Aucas. They were to have reported by radio again that afternoon.

Back at the mission station, five missionary wives waited for a call that never came. Five days later, their husbands' speared and mutilated bodies were found in the muddy river by a rescue team.

A shocked world responded in various ways to the news. Some questioned the priorities of these five brilliant young men. Why would they leave the comfort and pleasure of the United States to go to such a remote and dangerous mission field? (Many still ask that question of missionaries today.) Some were angry at the mission board—and at God—for allowing this "unnecessary waste of life." (Some people still berate the folly of such "wasted money and effort.") Others were convinced that this once again proved the futility of serving a mythical God who will not even protect his own faithful workers. (There are those who still use this kind of argument against purposeful suffering.)

Life magazine covered the story with news and photographs giving complete details of the deaths. A rash of letters were written to the editor. Many appeared in the "Letters to the Editor" column. They were filled with both bitter and sympathetic reactions. "Why did they die?" asked people in tones of resentment, criticism, and sorrow.

At my desk in Fort Worth, Texas, where I was a student in seminary, I, too, read the news and asked the question, "Why?"

Then, as if God had spoken to me verbally, the answer came back: "Why? Watch and see!" And from that day on I did watch. I became acutely aware of the many things that began to happen as a direct result of this tragedy.

First, mission causes were advanced all around the world as a result of the sacrifice of these five young men. Millions of dollars poured into mission treasuries. Thousands of young people were stirred, and surrendered their lives to God's service.

Next, the Auca Indians were reached—by, of all people, Rachel Saint and Betty Elliot. The entire tribe was eventually won to a saving knowledge of the Lord Jesus Christ. One of the Auca men directly responsible for the death of the missionaries became a minister of the gospel among his people.

The blessings continued. They will never end! However, may I mention two more? At the time of the missionaries' deaths, my son was only eleven years old. In 1961, he surrendered his life to the ministry. When asked the one thing that influenced him most in his decision, he replied, "Reading the books: *Jungle Pilot, Through Gates of Splendor,* and *Shadow of the Almighty*"—books written about the five missionaries.

Years later, I went through a trying experience and the testing of my own faith. By reading these same three books I was brought safely through the "fire" of doubt.

"Why did they die?" Tragedy or triumph? What do you think? I know my answer. For I have both seen and heard the "meshing of gears."

Notes

Introduction

1. A phrase made popular by Samuel Taylor Coleridge in his poem, *The Ancient Mariner.* It refers to the bearing of a heavy burden, usually placed there by someone else. "Bearing a cross" is sometimes used in the same way to describe one's suffering, but this is not the true meaning of the passage in the New Testament. Jesus uses the term to describe obedience to God's will and death to self-will, even if it leads to suffering and a cross.

Chapter 2

1. William Shakespeare (1564-1616), *Macbeth.* Scene 5, lines 17-29

2. John Dryden (1631-1700), "To My Honor'd Friend Sir Robert Howard, on His Excellent Poems," lines 29-32. Published 1661.

3. Sidney J. Harris, *Strictly Personal* (Hall Syndicate, Inc., 1965).

4. One of the meanings of the Hebrew word for Satan.

5. Another meaning for the Hebrew word for Satan.

6. One of the meanings of the Greek word *diabolos,* usually translated *devil.*

7. Another meaning for the word *devil.*

8. Since Jesus retained his resurrected body, some have said that his wounds will be the only man-made things in heaven. If so, they will be a constant reminder of the price God was willing to pay to show his love and the evil of rebellion.

Chapter 3

1. Leprosy was imported to Hawaii in 1840 by Chinese laborers, where it soon found a fertile field among the Polynesians, who having no prior exposure to the disease, had built up no immunity.

In 1865 the first leper patients were transported to the island of Molokai on orders of King Kamehameha. They were located on a small desolate fourteen-square-mile peninsula jutting out like a triangle from the north side of the main island. Very little in the way of supplies, building material, and food was provided to the first unfortunate victims who were isolated on this volcanic island.

2. There are some slight variations to the story concerning the details of Father Damien's discovery of leprosy in his own body and the words of his announcement to his people. But the actual account is factual. It is not known for sure where or when or how Father Damien contracted leprosy, but he died from the disease in 1889. Other than Father Damien, no one else working with the patients has ever developed the disease because of their contact with them.

Chapter 5

1. C. S. Lewis, *The Problem of Pain* (New York: The Macmillan Co., 1970), pp. 93,95.

2. Edward Mote (1797-1874), "The Solid Rock."

3. A. Graham Ikin, *Victory Over Suffering* (Great Neck, NY: Channel Press, 1956), pp. 24,36.

4. From "Higher Ground" by Johnson Oatman, Jr.

Chapter 6

1. Leslie D. Weatherhead, *Why Do Men Suffer?* (Nashville: Abingdon Press, 1936), p. 57.

Chapter 7

1. Napoleon Hill and W. Clement Stone, *Success Through a Positive Mental Attitude* (Englewood Cliffs, NJ: Prentice-Hall, Inc., 1960), pp. 80-81.

2. Ella Wheeler Wilcox (1855-1919), "The Winds of Fate."

3. Hill and Stone, *Success Through a Positive Mental Attitude*, p. 6.

Chapter 8

1. "Life's Problems" by Irvin H. Cady. Used by permission from *The Exchangite*, September 1976.

2. Peter Marshall (ed. Catherine Marshall), *Mr. Jones, Meet the Master* (New York: Fleming H. Revell, 1949), pp. 172-75. Used by permission of Chosen Books.

3. "From Along the Road" by Robert Browning Hamilton.

4. A prayer given by Peter Marshall while serving as a senate chaplain. Used by permission Chosen Books.

Chapter 9

1. From "The Giaour" by Lord Byron.

2. Edward FitzGerald, *The Rubáiyát of Omar Khayyám*.

3. John Greenleaf Whittier, *Maud Muller*.

4. Francis Brett Harte (1836-1902), "Mrs. Judge Jenkins: Sequel to Maud Muller."

5. From Ann Landers. Field Newspaper Syndicate, *Daily Report*, Ontario, CA. Used by permission.

6. Through political intervention by our government, the young man has been released and is back in the United States, living near San Francisco. His health was impaired from the many months of privation and confinement under unsanitary conditions, but he has now regained much of his health.

Chapter 10

1. Each year thousands of seemingly healthy babies die in their sleep from Sudden Infant Death Syndrome (SIDS). They are tucked into their beds only to be found dead a few hours later, leaving empty cribs, tiny graves, and broken hearts.

There is still no known cause, prevention, treatment, or cure for this strange phenomenon. It is unpredictable, and as far as is known, unpreventable. The parents are completely blameless, and totally helpless in the face of this tragedy.

There is some indication that SIDS may go back as far as biblical times. A veiled reference is made to it in 1 Kings 3:13 where the word *overlaid* is used.

2. From Arthur John Gossip, "The Hero in Thy Soul," based on Jer. 12:5 (New York: Charles Scribner's Sons, 1933), pp. 110-111.

Chapter 11

1. Perhaps this is an unusual chapter to be included in a book on suffering. However, the subject deserves our attention since a negative self-image or a feeling of unworthiness can be very painful and self-destructive.

2. Institute of Basic Youth Conflicts, 1027 Arlington Avenue, La Grange, IL 60525. Introduction to Part one, *Self Image, Acceptance of Self.*

3. Much of the Bible deals with suffering: Individual, tribal, national, and even divine. But the Book of Job is unique since it is the only book concerned with the problem as its main theme.

4. The original prayer is credited to Saint Francis of Assisi.

5. James K. Van Fleet, *Power with People* (West Nyack, NY: Parker, 1970), pp. 198-99.

6. Hill and Stone, *Success Through a Positive Mental Attitude*, pp. 19-20.

Chapter 12

1. From *Decision.* Copyright 1965 by the Billy Graham Evangelistic Association. Used by permission.

Bibliography

Bakan, David. *Disease, Pain, & Sacrifice*. Chicago: The University of Chicago Press, 1968.

Browker, John. *Problems of Suffering in Religions of the World*. Cambridge: Cambridge University Press, 1970.

Chambers, Oswald. *The Shadow of an Agony*. London: Simpkin Marshall Ltd., 1941.

DeHaan, M. R. *Broken Things*. Grand Rapids: Zondervan Publishing House, 1948.

De Pressense, E. *The Mystery of Suffering and Other Discourses*. New York: Carlton and Lanahan, 1869.

Dodd, Paul R. *When Life Tumbles In, What Then?* New York: Carlton Press, Inc., 1970.

Everly, Louis. *Suffering*. New York: Herder and Herder, 1967.

Ferre, Nels F. S. *Evil and the Christian Faith*. New York: Harper & Brothers, 1947.

Fitch, William. *God & Evil*. Grand Rapids: William B. Eerdmans Publishing Company, 1967.

Gothard, Bill. *Institute in Basic Youth Conflicts, Self Image*. La Grange, IL: Author, 1969.

Guillebaud, H. E. *Some Moral Difficulties of the Bible*. London: Inter-Varsity Fellowship, 1941.

Hall, Charles Cuthbert. *Does God Send Trouble?* Boston: Houghton, Mifflin, and Company, 1894.

Heath, Thomas R. *In Face of Anguish*. New York: Sheed and Ward, Inc., 1966.

Hill, Napoleon and Keown, E. Harold. *Succeed and Grow Rich Through Persuasion*. New York: Fawcett World Library, 1970.

Hill, Napoleon and Stone, W. Clement. *Success Through a Positive Mental Attitude*. Englewood Cliffs, NJ: Prentice-Hall, Inc., 1960.

Hobbs, Herschel H. *When the Rain Falls*. Grand Rapids: Baker Book House, 1967.

Ikin, Graham A. *Victory Over Suffering*. Great Neck, NY: Channel Press, Inc., 1956.

Jones, E. Stanley. *Christ and Human Suffering*. New York: The Abingdon Press, 1933.

Kierkegaard, Soren. *The Concept of Dread?* Princeton: Princeton University Press, 1957.

Kubler-Ross, Elisabeth. *On Death and Dying*. London: The Macmillan Company, 1969.

Lewis, C. S. *The Problem of Pain*. New York: The Macmillan Company, 1970.

Maltz, Maxwell. *Psycho-Cybernetics.* Englewood Cliffs, NJ: Prentice-Hall, Inc., 1960.

Maltz, Maxwell. *Creative Living for Today.* New York: Trident Press, 1967.

Marshall, Catherine. *Beyond Our Selves.* New York: McGraw-Hill Book Company, Inc., 1961.

Marshall, Peter (Marshall, Catherine). *Mr. Jones Meets the Master.* Westwood, NJ: Fleming H. Revell Co., 1950.

Maston, T. B. *Suffering: A Personal Perspective.* Nashville: Broadman Press, 1967.

Oates, Wayne E. *The Revelation of God in Human Suffering.* Philadelphia: The Westminister Press, 1959.

Peake, Arthur Samuel. *The Problem of Suffering in the Old Testament.* London: Primitive Methodist Publishing House, 1904.

Peale, Norman Vincent. *The Healing of Sorrow.* Pawling, NY: Inspirational Book Service, 1966.

Petit, Francois. *The Problem of Evil.* New York: Hawthorn Books, 1959.

Petrie, Asenath. *Individuality in Pain and Suffering.* Chicago: The University of Chicago Press, 1967.

Pickford, J. H. *Gethsemane.* London: Marshall, Morgan & Scott, Ltd.

Proudfoot, Merrill. *Suffering: A Christian Understanding.* Philadelphia: The Westminister Press, 1964.

Reed, Elizabeth L. *Helping Children with the Mystery of Death.* Nashville: Abingdon Press, 1970.

Robinson, H. Wheeler. *The Religious Ideas of the Old Testament.* London: Duckworth, 1913.

Smith, Helen Reagan. *Jesus Stood by Us.* Nashville: Broadman Press, 1970.

Switzer, David K. *The Dynamics of Grief.* Nashville: Abingdon Press, 1970.

Van Fleet, James K. *Power with People.* West Nyack, NY: Parker Publishing Co., Inc., 1970.

Weatherhead, Leslie D. *Salute to a Sufferer.* Nashville: Abingdon Press, 1962.

Weatherhead, Leslie D. *Why Do Men Suffer?* New York: Abingdon-Cokesbury Press, 1936.